PHRASAL VERB ORGANISER

with Mini-Dictionary

JOHN FLOWER

Editor: Jimmie Hill

LTP

LANGUAGE TEACHING PUBLICATIONS
35 Church Road, Hove BN3 2BE

ISBN 0 906717 62 0
© **LTP 1993**
Reprinted 1993

The Author

John Flower is a teacher at Eurocentre Bournemouth where he has worked for many years. He has long experience of teaching Cambridge examination classes for whom phrasal verbs are a serious problem. He is the author of the popular **Build Your Vocabulary** series. His first book in LTP's Organiser series was **First Certificate Organiser**.

Personal Note

The author would like to express his thanks to Jimmie Hill and Michael Lewis for coming up with ideas; to his students and colleagues at Eurocentre for trying out the exercises; and to Ruth, Helen, and Andrew for their special contribution.

Acknowledgements

Cover design by Anna Macleod.
Illustrations by Martin Cater, Anna Macleod, Pantelis Palios and Michael Salter.
Typeset by Blackmore Typesetting Services, Brighton.
Printed in England by Commercial Colour Press, London E7.

Using This Book

There are thousands of phrasal verbs in English. Some are very common. Some are rare. Some have more than one meaning. This book practises over 700 with more than 1,000 meanings.

Phrasal verbs can be organised

This book organises them in different ways – by particle, by verb, and by topic. The more different ways you meet these verbs, the more you will learn.

If you are learning English in class

Your teacher can only spend a small amount of time teaching you phrasal verbs. You must spend time at home learning them for yourself. The more you study at home, the better your English will become.

If you are learning English on your own without a teacher

It is better to do a little at regular intervals, rather than a lot at one time, and then nothing for weeks.

If you do not understand the meaning of a verb

Do not worry! See if the context of the verb can help you to understand its meaning. Look the verb up in the Mini-Dictionary at the back of this book or in your own dictionary. Study the example and try to write your own sentence using the verb. This will help you to remember what the verb means and how it is used.

If you are studying for an examination

You can use the special organising pages and Your Personal List at the end of the book. Cover part of the page and test yourself.

Contents

5

Getting Started

1 What is a phrasal verb?

A phrasal verb is a verb plus one or two particles.

Here are some common verbs: **bring, get, go, put, take, turn.**

Here are some common particles: **up, down, out, in, off, on**.
Some teachers call them prepositions or adverbs, but it is
easier to think of them as all 'particles'.

Here are some examples of phrasal verbs:

bring in   go off
take out   get on with

To understand what a phrasal verb is, let us look
at the verb GET:

GET as an ordinary verb:

Can you get me a glass of milk?

**GET with one or two particles
to form phrasal verbs:**

GET IN: The window was open. A thief got
in and stole the video . (enter)

GET ON WITH: We don't get on with our neighbours. (We aren't friendly to each
other.)
Please get on with your work. (Please continue with your work.)

"I don't think they get on very well."

*You can see that some phrasal verbs are easy, and some are more difficult to
understand. Working through the exercises in this book will help you understand
these verbs and their meanings.*

2 Where does the particle go?

**Very often the particle comes immediately
after the verb, but this is not always true.**

Particle immediately after the verb:
The cat stayed on top of the wall and only got
down at meal times. (descend)

Particle after the object:
This terrible weather is getting many people down.
(making them depressed)

Particle before or after the object:
Did you get down all the information?
(manage to make a note of it)
Did you get all the information down?

"I'm getting wet. It's getting me down."

If the object is a pronoun, the particle comes after: Did you get it down?

3 Identifying phrasal verbs

There are thousands of phrasal verbs in English. Here is an exercise to help you discover and learn these verbs as you study English.

Look at these extracts from three articles. There are twelve phrasal verbs. Underline them and write them on the lines beside the texts.

Smoke from the fire in the kitchen set a fire alarm off. Mr and Mrs Newton and their two children managed to get out through a window. One man in the flats upstairs was watching TV and hadn't realised what was happening. He had the shock of his life when firemen broke in and told him to leave immediately.

1. _____
2. _____
3. _____

Annoyed by telephone salespeople? Don't put up with them any longer! Whenever one rings you up, you should ask them to hold on because you have to consult someone. You then simply carry on doing what you were doing before. When you return after about ten minutes, you should find that the caller has hung up.

4. _____
5. _____
6. _____
7. _____
8. _____

We needed money to pay off the loan so I decided never to turn down any jobs that I was offered. Of course the work piled up and I just couldn't do it all. My wife was worried that I was going to crack up and started helping me when she could.

9. _____
10. _____
11. _____
12. _____

Did you understand those twelve verbs? If not, check in the Mini-Dictionary at the end of this book.

When you read a new text, find the phrasal verbs. Check to see if they are included in the Mini-Dictionary. If not, make your own list of verbs. There are some special pages at the end of the book to help you do this.

Match each phrasal verb from the previous exercise with its correct definition. Use each verb once only. See how many verbs you can remember without looking back at the exercise.

1. .... If you ....an alarm, for example, you cause it to start.

2. .... If you're in a building where there is danger and you .... , you manage to escape.

3. .... When firemen come to a house and .... , they enter it using force.

4. .... If you .... someone or something, you tolerate them.

5. .... If you .... someone ...., you phone them.

6. .... If you ask someone to ...., you want them to wait.

7. .... If you .... doing something, you continue doing it.

8. .... You .... when you end a phone conversation.

9. .... If you .... a loan, you pay the money you owe.

10. .... If you .... the offer of a job, you say you don't want it.

11. .... If work ...., you have too much to do.

12. .... When people are under a lot of pressure and ...., they have a nervous breakdown.

Did you notice how the phrasal verb 'set off' was used? Note the combination:

set a fire alarm off

Look back at the opposite page and find the nouns which go with the following:

"I didn't set it off. It went off by itself!"

.... **has hung up**

turn down ....

.... **piled up**

It is important to note down any common partnerships that verbs form with nouns. This will help you to understand and remember the phrasal verbs you meet.

9

4 **What do phrasal verbs mean?**

It is often possible to understand what a phrasal verb means by looking at its particle. As you do the exercises in this book, try to notice patterns of meaning and build up lists based on these patterns. Although it is not always possible to find a pattern, thinking about the meaning of the particle will help you to understand and remember the phrasal verbs you meet.

Below you will see some of the meanings of the six most common particles used with phrasal verbs.

UP

An upward movement:
We left early, just as the sun was coming up.

An increase, an improvement:
Sales have gone up in the past year.

Completing, ending:
We used up all the eggs when we made the cake.

Approaching:
A taxi drew up just as we were thinking of calling one.

"Sales are UP!"

DOWN

A downward movement:
The teacher told the pupils to sit down.

A decrease:
That music is too loud! Turn it down!

Completing, ending, stopping:
Business was so bad that the shop had to close down.

"Turn it DOWN!"

OUT

An outward movement, not being inside:
Let's eat out this evening.

Excluding:
The double glazing helps to shut out the noise.

Completing, doing thoroughly:
It took me hours to clean out that room.

IN/INTO

An inward movement:
The spectators poured into the stadium.

Including, being involved:
We'd better let her into the secret.

"Next week, you can clean it OUT!"

10

OFF

Movement away, detaching:
We set off at midday.

Preventing entry, separating, not including:
They've fenced off their garden to keep dogs out.

"We can't get IN – they've fenced it OFF to keep us OUT!"

ON

Touching, attaching:
I wish you wouldn't put on so much lipstick!

Continuing:
He went on talking as if nothing had happened.

The other particles can often be understood because they have their literal meanings of place or movement. Here are some additional meanings:

"He just went ON talking – as if nothing had happened!"

AWAY

Continuous activity:
The secretary kept typing away, ignoring the noise outside.

BACK

Returning:
I've given back the tools I borrowed.

Reference to past time:
This photo brings back memories of when I was young.

THROUGH

Completing, doing thoroughly:
I need to think this through before I decide.

"It brings BACK memories!"

When you read or hear a phrasal verb that you have ever met before, try to guess its meaning. Does its particle help you to understand it? Can you guess its meaning from its context?
Look the verb up in a dictionary to see if you are correct. Make a note of the verb and write your own sentence so that you can remember the meaning.

Verbs with UP – 1

1 Complete each of the sentences with the correct form of one of the verbs below and the particle UP. Use each verb once only.

build cheer grow liven put shoot speak stand

1. I'm not tall enough to reach. Can you .... this poster for me?

2. Why are you so miserable? .... ! Things can't be that bad!

3. When the headmaster came in, most of the pupils .... but a few remained seated.

4. The party was really boring so I suggested some games to .... it ....

5. After a long illness, it takes some time to .... your strength.

6. She's a bit deaf so you'll have to ....

7. I was born in Washington but I .... in New York.

8. The weather's been so bad that the price of strawberries has ....

The 'UP' in the verbs in this exercise had the meaning of an upward movement, an increase or an improvement.

"Could you speak up, John!"

2 Now do the same with these verbs:

fill heal hurry lock ring save seal tidy

1. Why are you walking so slowly? We'll have to .... or we'll be late.

2. You've got my number so you can .... me .... if you have any problems.

3. It was a deep wound so it took some time to ....

4. It's a long journey so remember to .... the petrol tank before you go.

5. If you're worried about things falling out of the parcel, you'd better use some strong tape to .... it ....

6. He was such a dangerous prisoner that they .... him .... in a room and put a guard outside.

7. She was finally able to buy the bicycle after she'd .... enough money.

8. You'll be able to find everything if you .... your room.

In exercise 2 it is possible to omit 'UP' from each sentence. Sometimes it appears to intensify the verb it follows.

Verbs with UP – 2

1 **Match one half of the dialogue on the left with the other half on the right. Write your answers in the boxes.**

1. Why are they so tired this morning?

   A Well, I didn't make it, so don't expect me to clear it up!

2. Why have you set your alarm for five o'clock?

   B Of course! I'll back you up. Let's go and see the manager.

3. Joe's missed a lot of lessons.

   C I'm afraid not. I've used it all up.

4. Lucy's very polite, isn't she?

   D Of course not. You'll have to dress up.

5. Look at the mess all over the floor!

   E Yes. It'll be very hard for him to catch up.

6. Can I wear jeans this evening?

   F Because I have to get up early.

7. Will you support me if I complain about the food?

   G Because they stayed up late watching television.

8. Is there any milk left?

   H Yes. She's been very well brought up.

1		2		3		4		5		6		7		8	

2 **Now do the same with these dialogues:**

1. I don't know which one is which. Do you?

   A No, drink up! It's time to go.

2. Can I have an ice-cream?

   B Yes. They've blown up the Central Bank.

3. I can't understand this word.

   C Only if you eat up all your vegetables.

4. My French isn't very good.

   D All right. And I'll wash up afterwards.

5. Have you heard about the terrorist attack?

   E Why don't you go to evening classes to brush up?

6. What shall I do about this letter asking for money?

   F No. It's very easy to mix them up, isn't it?

7. Shall we have another drink?

   G Well look it up!

8. Would you like me to cook the meal this evening?

   H I'd tear it up if I were you.

1		2		3		4		5		6		7		8	

Now go through the sentences on the right and underline the phrasal verbs.

Verbs with UP – 3

1 **Complete each sentence with the correct form of one of the verbs given and the particle UP. Use each verb once only.**

beat call crop light own pull speed split

1. At first the coach went quite slowly but it began to .... as we got onto the motorway.

2. The fireworks exploded in all their colours and ....the sky.

3. The phone never stopped ringing as her friends kept .... her .... to congratulate her .

4. It was a really violent attack. The robbers .... him .... so badly that he had to be treated in hospital.

5. The car suddenly came towards us. It................................. in front of the store and Andre Agassi got out!

6. I won't be able to go out tonight because a problem has just ....

7. If the person who broke the window doesn't ...., the whole class will be punished.

"I was badly beaten up, as you can see."

8. Over sixty people arrived to help look for the missing girl. They .... into groups of four or five and went off in different directions.

2 **Now do the same with these verbs:**

bottle dig freshen polish screw tighten

1. The press are always looking for scandal. They're trying to ....information about his past.

2. You could tell that she wasn't happy about the news by the way she .... her face in disapproval.

3. He hasn't spoken Spanish for ages so he wants to .... it .... before his holiday.

4. I can tell you're upset. Don't ....your feelings. It'll only make things worse.

5. That's the third break-in this month. We must .... security to prevent any more.

6. Where's the ladies' room? I need to .... before we go into the restaurant.

Verbs with UP – 4

1 **Match a number with a letter. Use each item once only. Write your answers in the boxes.**

1. do up	A appearances although he'd lost all his money.
2. fold up	B the bank and steal a hundred thousand pounds.
3. hold up	C the volume so that we can all hear.
4. keep up	D the letter and put it in the envelope.
5. kick up	E your overcoat because it's cold.
6. stir up	F the situation in a few words.
7. sum up	G trouble for the rest of us.
8. turn up	H a fuss about the room being so cold.

"Brrr. I'd better do up my jacket."

1		2		3		4		5		6		7		8	

2 **Now do the same with these sentences:**

1. The caller	A broke up and we all went home.
2. A car	B froze up so she couldn't open the door.
3. The contestants	C flared up and some people were hurt.
4. The lock	D drew up and the driver got out.
5. The party	E hung up before I could ask him his name.
6. Violence	F lined up and paraded in front of the judges.
7. The windows	G piled up while I was away on holiday.
8. Work	H misted up and we couldn't see outside.

1		2		3		4		5		6		7		8	

Test yourself by covering one column and trying to remember the other part.

15

Verbs with UP – 5

1 Complete each sentence with the correct form of one of the verbs given and the particle UP. Use each verb once only.

come   give   go   make   pick   put   set   take

1. The hotels were all full so we offered to .... Carla .... for the night.

2. Early that morning, we set off on our journey as the sun was ....

3. An enquiry was .... into the use of chemicals in farming.

4. You're such a good singer that you should ....
   it .... professionally.

5. Are you coming or not? Please .... your
   mind!

6. We managed to escape before the factory
   .... in flames.

7. Do you know any Turkish?
   I .... a bit while I was on holiday in
   Istanbul.

8. Tony's free time was very important to him and he
   resented having to .... some of it ....
   to help with the shopping.

"It went up in flames before we could put it out."

2 Now do the same with these verbs:

come   give   go   make   pick   put   set   take

1. I've decided to .... your offer of a part-time job.

2. As the home team came out onto the field a cheer .... from their
   supporters.

3. He was supposed to be a very violent man but he didn't .... much of a
   fight when the police finally caught him.

4. Where do you want me to put the computer and printer?
   – Could you .... them ....in that corner?

5. I'll give you a lift. If you wait on the corner, I'll .... you .... at 6 o'clock.

6. When they realised that nobody could possibly have survived the explosion they decided
   to .... the search.

7. Was that story true, or was she ....it all .... ?

8. Has Isabelle said anything about me?
   – Well your name ....in the course of conversation last night.

Organising Verbs with UP – 1

Complete each of the groups of sentences below with one of the following verbs. Use each verb once only.

| | come up | go up | pick up | set up |
| | give up | make up | put up | take up |

1.

Did he		a prize at the show?
Does he expect me to		the bill?
I managed to		some ideas at the meeting.

2.

I'll have to		my job and look after her.
If you		smoking, you'll feel better.
Tommy,		your seat to the lady!

3.

Won't it		too much of your time?
She decided to		her skirt as it was too long.
I think I'll		golf, when I retire.

4.

Don't		an excuse! Tell the truth!
Will they ever		their quarrel?
Come on! You must		your mind!

5.

They've		an enquiry into the incident.
You need money to		in business.
The police		road blocks to stop the terrorists.

6.

I've been forced to		prices.
He's agreed to		the money you need.
The party may		an alternative candidate.

7.

We watched the moon		over the hill.
Did the subject		in the course of conversation?
People used to		and speak to her.

8.

Prices will		in the New Year.
We saw the building		in flames.
Why don't you		and introduce yourself?

Test yourself by covering the middle column.

Organising Verbs with UP – 2

Fill each blank with one of the following verbs. Use each verb once only.

break up	**draw up**	**hold up**	**look up**
bring up	**get up**	**keep up**	**turn up**

1.
You must		Don't walk so slowly.
I hope this rain doesn't		much longer.
We try to		appearances.

2.
It was tactless to		such a sensitive subject.
She had to		the children alone.
Why don't you		the matter of expenses.

3.
If you		your collar, you won't be so cold.
It's too soft. Please		the volume.
They didn't		until the party was over.

4.
It will take time to		an agreement.
We saw a car		and a man get out.
Why don't you		your chair nearer to the fire?

5.
Things are beginning to		at last.
He didn't even		when he came in.
Remember to		any words you don't know.

6.
If you know the answer		your hand.
The robbers planned to		the bank in the town centre.
The police had to		the traffic because of the accident.

7.
It'll take ages to		that hill!
I have to		early tomorrow morning.
We should		a petition against the motorway.

8.
The ship began to		on the rocks.
The police decided to		the meeting.
When do the schools		for the summer holiday?

Test yourself by covering the phrasal verbs.

Organising Verbs with UP – 3

Complete the blanks in the definitions with the verbs below. Use each verb once only.

back	brush	dig	screw	beat
cheer	freshen	stay	blow	crop
mix	tighten	bottle	dress	own

1. .... **up**   If children .... to watch television, they don't go to bed at the normal time.

2. .... **up**   People who .... their emotions try to control them and not show how they are feeling.

3. .... **up**   If you tell someone to ...., you want them to stop being so miserable.

4. .... **up**   If you .... to something wrong, you admit you were the person who did it.

5. .... **up**   When terrorists .... a bridge, they destroy it with an explosion.

6. .... **up**   People who .... you .... hit or kick you and hurt you badly.

7. .... **up**   When you ...., you wash and make yourself look more presentable.

8. .... **up**   If you .... to go to a party, you wear very smart clothes.

9. .... **up**   If you .... two people or things, you can't tell the difference between them.

10. .... **up**   When you .... your Spanish, you improve it.

11. .... **up**   If you .... your face, you twist a part of it to show disapproval.

12. .... **up**   When you .... someone ...., you give them help and support.

13. .... **up**   When you .... security, you make it stricter.

14. .... **up**   Problems which .... appear unexpectedly.

15. .... **up**   If you .... information, you discover something that had been kept secret.

To test yourself cover the sentence and try to remember how the verb is used.

Verbs with DOWN – 1

1 Complete each sentence with the correct form of one of the verbs given and the particle DOWN. Use each verb once only.

blow   chop   kneel   lie   pour   shoot   sit   slow

1. Make yourself at home. .... I'll be with you in a moment.

2. I feel a bit tired so I think I'll .... for a while.

3. You'd better take your umbrella because it's ....

4. You're driving too fast! .... or you'll have an accident!

5. The tree was dying so we had to .... it ....

6. Tall people can be very frightening for small children. If you're tall, ... when you're speaking to them so that you're at their level.

7. It was very windy last night and several trees were ....

8. Did you hear on the news that a UN plane was .... this morning?

"Kneel down or bend down when you speak to children. Get down to their level!"

2 Now do the same with these verbs:

calm   cool   cut   fall   mark   quieten   tear   tone

1. This coffee's too hot! I'll wait until it has .... before I drink it.

2. There's no need to get so excited! Try to .... !

3. If they saw any posters with his picture on, the protestors .... them ....

4. If you can't give up smoking entirely, at least try to ....

5. Everyone started talking at once. Finally, after they had ...., he continued speaking.

6. The church tower was damaged in the storm and a week later, it ....

7. During the sale some prices were .... by as much as 50 per cent.

8. So as not to cause offence they asked her to .... her speech.

Did you notice that the verbs in these exercises had the idea of a downward movement or some kind of reduction or decrease?

Verbs with DOWN - 2

1 **Match one half of the dialogue on the left with the other half on the right. Write your answers in the boxes.**

1. I hate these pills!

2. I want to travel and see the world.

3. My hair keeps sticking up.

4. We haven't finished decorating the spare bedroom yet.

5. How long do you think the dispute will last?

6. Joannna seems to be under a lot of stress.

7. What happened when they found out they were wrong?

8. Are my football boots up there?

A Your friends will just have to bed down in the living room, then, won't they?

B They had to climb down and admit they'd made a mistake.

C Yes. Shall I throw them down to you?

D Come on! Swallow it down?

E I think she's feeling weighed down by all her responsibilities.

F If neither side backs down, it could go on for ages.

G Isn't it time you got a job and settled down?

H Use some water to smooth it down.

"Good boy! Swallow it down!"

1		2		3		4		5		6		7		8	

2 **Now do the same with these dialogues:**

1. Why is John so irritable these days?

2. I've got to make a speech and don't know what to say.

3. How do you manage to relax after a hard day at the office?

4. Where is the space shuttle going to land?

5. You will come, won't you?

6. How did the accident happen?

7. People still remember the time Jeremy put salt in his tea.

8. How old is that story?

A I don't know. It's been handed down from generation to generation.

B She was run down by a lorry while crossing the road.

C It's supposed to splash down somewhere in the Pacific.

D I think the constant noise is beginning to wear him down.

E I find yoga helps me to wind down.

F He'll never live it down, will he?

G Why don't you write down a few ideas first?

H Don't worry! I won't let you down.

1		2		3		4		5		6		7		8	

Now underline all the phrasal verbs in the exercises.

Verbs with DOWN – 3

1 **Complete each sentence with the correct form of one of the verbs given and the particle DOWN. Use each verb once only.**

copy   fall   get   keep   tie   tumble   water   wave

1. I'm so annoyed with myself for making a mistake!
   – You shouldn't let it .... you .... like this.

2. A teacher might see you if you put your head up!
   .... !

3. It's important to follow the instructions so
   .... the details carefully and
   check them when you've finished.

4. It's a very weak argument that ....
   on at least two points.

5. Ann can do what she likes. She has no family
   responsibilities to .... her ....

6. When the car broke down, we stood by the side of the
   road and managed to .... a passing
   motorist, who gave us a lift to town.

7. They didn't like the strong language in his speech and
   they asked him to .... it .... to avoid
   a diplomatic incident.

8. The boy took a tin from the bottom of the stack and the rest came ....

". . . and then they all came tumbling down!"

*Did you notice that the phrasal verb **get ... down**, as it is used in the first example, must have its object between the verb and particle? It is important to check where the object can go with transitive phrasal verbs and to make a note of any difficulties.*

2 **Now do the same with these verbs:**

flutter   jot   lay   narrow   play   scale

1. I'd better just .... those dates in case I forget.

2. The Soviets tried to .... the incident at Chernobyl. It was much more serious than they admitted at first.

3. We were starting to run out of money so we've had to .... our operations.

4. The regulations .... minimum safety standards in the workplace.

5. As I looked up, a piece of paper came .... from a window on the third floor.

6. Originally we had over fifty suspects but we've managed to .... them .... to five.

Notice in the last example the object comes between the verb and particle.

Verbs with DOWN – 4

1 **When you meet a phrasal verb, notice the noun it is used with. This will help you understand and remember the verb much better. Match an item on the right with an item on the left. Use each item once only. Write your answers in the boxes.**

1. The birds	A	beat down and we got very hot.
2. The building	B	broke down on the journey home.
3. The car	C	burnt down and all the contents were destroyed.
4. The noise	D	cracked down hard to prevent more violence.
5. The plane	E	died down and I was able to concentrate again.
6. The police	F	pelted down and they got extremely wet.
7. The rain	G	swooped down and took the breadcrumbs from the grass.
8. The sun	H	touched down at the airport two hours late.

1		2		3		4		5		6		7		8	

2 **Now do the same with these:**

1. batter down	A	the blinds if the sun gets too bright.
2. note down	B	your new address.
3. pull down	C	the door to get in.
4. set down	D	the information I was looking for.
5. shout down	E	minimum standards of hygiene.
6. slam down	F	the phone, looking very angry.
7. track down	G	the walls before you start painting.
8. wash down	H	the speaker so he's unable to continue.

"Please don't slam the phone down like that!"

1		2		3		4		5		6		7		8	

Test yourself by covering one of the columns.

Verbs with DOWN – 5

1 **Complete each sentence with the correct form of one of the verbs given and the particle DOWN. Use each verb once only.**

bring   come   go   hold   knock   put   take   turn

1. As my friend was crossing the road, she was .... by a speeding car.

2. The couple stood on the beach and watched the sun .... over the horizon.

3. The Opposition parties hope the scandal will................................ the President and his government.

4. Our dog was in such pain that we had him ....

5. Mary, there's someone on the phone with an urgent order. Can you .... it ...., please?

6. The prisoner became violent and it took 4 officers to .... him ....

7. Now we've moved to the country, why don't you .... and visit us some time?

8. The committee had very strong feelings about the kind of person who wasn't acceptable. They................................ any applicant who was wearing jeans, for example.

"Poor old Rover! We had to have him put down!"

2 **Now use the same verbs in these sentences. Notice how the verbs have completely different meanings.**

1. Land was needed for the new motorway and 100 houses were .... to make way for it.

2. We've spent hours putting up all the decorations. When the party's over, we'll have to .... them all .... again.

3. It's a bit chilly in here. They've .... the heating.

4. Just as we arrived, the sky went very black and the rain .... so heavily that we got extremely wet.

5. As you can imagine, the news of the team's defeat didn't .... very well.

6. The boss doesn't criticise other people like that. Why does he have to .... her .... all the time?

7. So Sid's unemployed again! He just can't .... a job for more than a few weeks!

8. The government is doing its best to .... the cost of houses so that more people can afford to buy a home of their own again.

Organising Verbs with DOWN – 1

Complete each group of sentences with one of the verbs below. Use each verb once only.

bring down	go down	knock down	take down
come down	hold down	put down	turn down

1.
We'll have to		that wall.
Two witnesses saw him		the pedestrian.
If you		the price. You'll sell them all.

2.
How could you		such an offer?
Shall I		the volume?
We will, of course.		any unsuitable applicants.

3.
How much must I		as a deposit?
Vets hate having to		pets – even if they are injured.
He tends to		who doesn't agree with him.

4.
They're fighting to		the government.
The new policy will		prices.
We saw the defender		their centre forward.

5.
It's time to		the Christmas decorations.
My secretary will		the details.
Can you help me to		the tent?

6.
He can't		a job for very long.
We've managed to		prices.
It took four men to		such a strong person.

7.
You must		to the country and visit us.
The fog has		and made driving dangerous.
We expect them to		in favour of the proposal.

8.
The swelling will		in a few days.
I want him to		on his knees and apologise!
The news didn't		very well.

Test yourself by covering the phrasal verbs.

Organising Verbs with DOWN – 2

Complete each group of sentences with one of the verbs below. Use each verb once only.

| break down | get down | lay down | run down |
| fall down | keep down | let down | wind down |

1.

You can't		all the people who are relying on you.
Someone has		my tyres!
I had to		the dress because it was too short.

2.

He might		if he climbs that tree.
The argument seems to		in several places.
The houses will		eventually if they aren't repaired.

3.

Don't let these problems	(you)	so much!
Did your secretary		everything that was said?
Please		out of that tree immediately!

4.

We had to		the door to get in.
Many people		because of the pressure of their work.
Did the car		on the motorway?

5.

Could you		the window and let some air into the car?
I find it hard to		after work?
We had to		the business and sack some of the staff.

6.

Why don't they		their guns and stop the fighting!
The regulations		minimum safety standards.
It's the young who mostly		their lives for their country.

7.

You must		! Someone might see you!
The boss wants to		costs as much as possible.
He used a wave of terror to		the entire population.

8.

She was		by a car while crossing the road.
Services are being		to save money.
If the batteries		the radio won't work so well.

Test yourself by covering the phrasal verbs.

Organising Verbs with DOWN – 3

Fill in the blanks in the definitions with the verbs below. Use each verb once only.

climb	play	tumble	crack	live
settle	water	hand	narrow	tie
wave	jot	pelt	track	wear

1. .... **down**   When you .... the choices, you reduce their number by eliminating the others.

2. .... **down**   When you .... a story, you pass it to the next generation.

3. .... **down**   Actions and circumstances that .... you .... make you weaker because of the constant pressure.

4. .... **down**   If it's difficult for you to .... something you did wrong, it means people won't forget it.

5. .... **down**   When you try to .... an incident............, you try to make it appear less important than it is.

6. .... **down**   If you have had a life where things kept changing and then ...., you live a life of stability and routine.

7. .... **down**   Normally you wouldn't want rain to .... as it would come down very heavily.

8. .... **down**   When the police ...., they enforce rules very strictly.

9. .... **down**   If circumstances .... you ...., they limit your freedom.

10. .... **down**   If you finally .... something you've been looking for, you find it after a lot of difficulty.

11. .... **down**   When tins etc ...., they fall down in disorder.

12. .... **down**   You .... a speech to make it weaker and less controversial.

13. .... **down**   When you .... someone driving past, you signal them to stop.

14. .... **down**   If people have an opinion about something and then ...., they admit that they were wrong.

15. .... **down**   When you .... information, you make a quick note of it.

Test yourself, by covering the right-hand side of the page.

Verbs with OUT – 1

1

Complete each sentence with the correct form of one of the verbs given and the particle OUT. Use each verb once only.

ask   cut   jump   keep   slip   squeeze   stay   walk

1. What he was saying made us so angry that we .... in protest.

2. As Jim was crossing the park, the mugger suddenly
   .... and attacked him.

3. There were guards at the front of the building to
   .... any protestors and stop them
   from disrupting the meeting.

4. How can I get Susan to go out with me?
   – You know she likes dancing so why don't you
   .... her .... to a disco?

5. If you want to lose weight, you'll have to
   .... everything sweet.

6. There's always some toothpaste left in the tube. I can
   never manage to .... that last bit ....

7. They didn't get home until six o'clock in the morning
   because they'd .... celebrating all night.

8. We don't want mum to notice us leaving. Leave the back door unlocked and we'll try to
   .... while she's watching television.

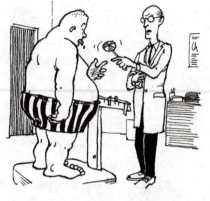

"No more lollipops! Cut out everything sweet!"

2

Now do the same with these verbs:

check   eat   leave   lock   pick   reach   rush   throw

1. Oh no! My keys are in the car! I think I've .... myself .... !

2. Why didn't you give your students any homework?
   – Because when the bell rang, they all .... before I had time to say anything.

3. Look through the wedding photos and .... any you'd like a copy of.

4. You need some shelves by your chair so that when you want a book, you can just
   .... and get it.

5. Look at the mess in here! Tidy your room and .... anything you don't need.

6. Rachel hadn't been playing well so they decided to .... her .... of the team.

7. My parents usually go to an Italian or Chinese restaurant when they ....

8. When they leave the hotel, guests are supposed to .... before eleven o'clock.

Did you notice that the verbs in the exercises had the meaning of an outward movement, being outside, or not including? Can you think of any more verbs like this with the particle OUT?

Verbs with OUT - 2

1 Match one half of the dialogue on the left with the other half on the right. Write your answers in the boxes.

1. Is there any chance of prices rising in the near future?

2. So we've got all the food. Any more problems?

3. So far only 20 people have written to say that they'll come.

4. What happened to your headlight?

5. I don't like the look of that man over there.

6. What do you think of Linda's pink and yellow T-shirt?

7. Why didn't Victor come as he'd promised?

8. Jane looks really relieved today.

A Me neither. Hey! Look out! He's got a knife!

B But we sent out more than 60 invitations!

C Well, she certainly stands out!

D Yes. She poured out all her problems to me last night.

E He caught some kind of virus and had to back out at the last moment.

F Yes. We've still got to sort out where everyone is going to sit.

"She certainly stands out in a crowd!"

G A car suddenly pulled out in front of mine and I ran into the back of it.

H I wouldn't rule out the possibility.

1		2		3		4		5		6		7		8	

2 Now do the same with these dialogues:

1. Isn't this grass too wet to have a picnic on?

2. Would you like another dance?

3. What should I do if I make a mistake?

4. It's a long journey and we could meet a lot of traffic.

5. I've spilt some wine on my jacket.

6. I want to ring Jean but I don't know if she's on the phone.

7. Rosemary looks really exhausted these days.

8. I don't want anyone to know I've been here.

A Why don't you find out by looking in the local directory?

B Try this. It'll wash out the stain.

C Do you mind if I sit this one out? My feet are killing me!

D Don't worry. I'll spread out this old blanket for us to sit on.

E I know. All that extra work is really tiring her out.

F I'll show you out through the back door. Nobody will see you.

G But if we set out early, we'll avoid the rush hour.

H Cross it out and write the correction above it.

1		2		3		4		5		6		7		8	

Now go through the sentences on the right and underline the phrasal verbs.

Verbs with OUT – 3

1 **Complete each of the sentences with the correct form of one of the verbs given and the particle OUT. Use each verb once only.**

camp   miss   pass   point   share   shut   storm   try

1. Everyone will get some if you .... the cake equally.

2. Ralph's just bought a tent and wants to .... in it for the night!

3. Excuse me, sir. We're asking for people's comments on this new fruit juice. Would you like to .... it .... ?

4. Please don't get the wrong idea. I must .... that this is the first accident we've had since the sports centre opened.

5. His secretary was so angry that she................................ and slammed the door behind her.

6. Some people can only cope with problems by .... them .... of their mind. I can't. I've got to come to terms with them.

7. It was so smoky and stuffy in the room that I nearly ....

8. Your essay is very good, but I'm afraid you've .... some rather important facts.

2 **Now do the same with these verbs:**

breathe   cry   hand   invite   measure   read   stretch   wear

1. Go on! .... her .... She's just waiting for you to ask her!

2. When Justin dropped the brick on his foot, we heard him .... in agony.

3. Could you ....the books now, please.

4. I've got to have a rest. Digging can really .... you ...., especially if you aren't used to it.

5. To make sure that everyone would hear she .... the names in a loud voice.

6. You've got to be very accurate when you do this. .... the powder carefully or the mixture will be too strong.

"Was that Justin crying out?"

7. Hold your breath for thirty seconds and then ....slowly through your nose.

8. I was so tired. All I wanted to do was .... on the sofa and go to sleep.

Verbs with OUT – 4

1 **Match a number with a letter to form a partnership. Use each item once only. Write your answers in the boxes.**

1. blow out   A   the answer, using a calculator.

2. burst out   B   the candle and leave the room in darkness.

3. call out   C   her cigarette in the ashtray.

4. carry out   D   the cupboard as we need more storage space.

5. clear out   E   the fire brigade to rescue my cat.

6. stub out   F   laughing because he looks so strange.

7. wear out   G   your good clothes if you wear them too often.

8. work out   H   a survey to see which soap people prefer.

"I didn't fall out. I bailed out."

1		2		3		4		5		6		7		8	

2 **Now do the same with these sentences:**

1. The bells   A   bailed out just before the plane exploded.

2. Some competitors   B   blared out and we couldn't hear each other speak.

3. The two friends   C   broke out by using an axe to smash the door.

4. Information   D   died out and nobody here knows anything about it.

5. The music   E   dropped out as the contest got more difficult.

6. The pilot   F   fell out and never spoke to each other again.

7. The prisoners   G   leaked out and stories appeared in the newspapers.

8. The tradition   H   rang out as the couple left the church.

1		2		3		4		5		6		7		8	

Verbs with OUT – 5

1 **Complete each of the sentences with the correct form of one of the verbs given and the particle OUT. Use each verb once only.**

come   give   go   let   make   put   take   turn

1. Usually this book can only be read in the library. You have to get special permission from the librarian if you want to .... it ....

2. It's a very bad stain. Are you sure this stuff will make it .... ?

3. I don't understand why boys think it's fun to .... their tongue .... at people!.

4. Every week this factory.............................. 2,000 new cars.

5. To get more publicity the organiser of the march printed some leaflets and .... them .... to people shopping in the market.

6. The prisoners are kept inside most of the time but they .... them .... for an hour every day so that they can get some exercise.

"Nasty little boys stick their tongues out!"

7. I was a very shy boy. I didn't .... with girls until I had left school.

8. Your grandfather isn't a very good actor. He tried to .... that he was deaf but he couldn't fool me!

2 **Now do the same with these sentences:**

1. As I had put on weight, my dress was too tight so I had to .... it............, especially around the waist.

2. Is there something wrong with this electric fire? It doesn't .... as much heat as it used to.

3. Despite all the problems we'd had, the event .... to be a great success.

4. I'm in agony! While I was lifting the piano, I .... my back ....

5. Put some more coal on the fire. It's ....

6. We knew hardly anything about her. The information about her double life only .... after her death.

7. It's all very suspicious. Mr Simpkins .... the insurance policy only a week before his wife died.

8. I didn't know which house I was looking for. It was too dark for me to .... the numbers.

Organising Verbs with OUT – 1

Complete each of the groups of sentences with one of the phrasal verbs below. Use each verb once only.

come out	**go out**	**make out**	**take out**
give out	**let out**	**put out**	**turn out**

1.

When does the film		in this country?
We watched the sun		from behind a cloud.
Can Billy		and play?

2.

My strength was starting to		when help finally arrived.
Can you		these books for me?
These electric fires		a lot of heat.

3.

He		an enormous sigh of relief.
I'll have to		this skirt.
We		the dogs to run round the garden.

4.

They		an appeal on the radio.
We need some water to		the fire.
I		my arm to stop myself falling.

5.

Everything will		all right in the end.
Could you		the light for me?
Did many people		to watch the procession?

6.

Does the tide		as far as those rocks?
We watched the lights		all over town.
I've got to		now but I'll be back for lunch.

7.

Please		the cheque to my husband.
I can't		what he's saying.
She tried to		that she didn't understand.

8.

You can		up to four books from the library.
I had to		a loan to pay for the car.
I would love to	(you)	for a really expensive meal!

Test yourself by covering the phrasal verbs.

Organising Verbs with OUT – 2

Complete each group of sentences with one of the verbs below. Use each verb once only.

break out	carry out	fall out	set out
call out	drop out	point out	work out

1.

If you		early, you'll miss the rush hour.
We		to create a new kind of magazine.
The food was		on tables in the garden.

2.

I can't		the answer to this sum.
Let's hope things will		all right in the end.
They		once a day to keep fit.

3.

Will he		his threat and dismiss us all?
We intend to		a survey into eating habits.
Please		my instructions precisely.

4.

I want you to		the answer if you know it.
We've had to		the police twice this week.
The union may		all the members on strike.

5.

A terrible forest fire will		if we don't stop people camping.
Fighting could		again if a solution isn't found.
The prisioners tried to		during the night.

6.

Most children's baby teeth		before they are 12.
How can two friends		over something so unimportant?
His hair began to		because of all the worry.

7.

The guide will		the famous buildings.
You must		that there isn't much time left.
I'd be grateful if you'd		all my mistakes.

8.

A few competitors may		if the race gets too tough.
Many students		before the end of their course.
A lot of slang words		of the language after a few years.

Organising Verbs with OUT – 3

Complete the blanks in the definitions with the verbs below. Use each verb once only.

back	find	pass	burst	hand
pick	spread	cross	invite	share
stand	cry	look	throw	storm

1. .... **out**   If you .... someone ...., you ask them to go out with you.

2. .... **out**   When you .... sweets, you divide them so that everyone gets some.

3. .... **out**   Cyclists should wear something bright so that they .... in the dark.

4. .... **out**   When you .... tickets etc, you distribute them.

5. .... **out**   When you .... someone ...., you order them out in anger.

6. .... **out**   When you .... a blanket etc, you open it and put it on a surface.

7. .... **out**   If you promise to do something and then ...., you don't keep your promise.

"He's crying out, but I can't make out what he's saying."

8. .... **out**   If you .... information, you learn or discover something you didn't know before.

9. .... **out**   When you tell someone to ...., you want them to be careful.

10. .... **out**   If you .... someone ...., you choose them.

11. .... **out**   If you .... a mistake, you put a line through it.

12. .... **out**   People who .... make a loud noise of pain or fear.

13. .... **out**   If you .... of a place, you leave in a very bad temper.

14. .... **out**   If a room is stuffy and you ...., you lose consciousness.

15. .... **out**   When you .... laughing or crying, you do this suddenly.

Verbs with INTO – 1

1 **Complete each verb with the correct form of one of the verbs given and the particle INTO. Use each verb once only.**

bump   burst   come   go   grow   rush   talk   tune

1. When her uncle died, Stephanie .... a lot of money.

2. Take your time. You should never .... important decisions.

3. My boss has been trying to .... me .... having a holiday, but I've got too much work.

4. When I want to listen to the news, I usually .... my local radio station.

5. She was walking through the park when she................................. an old friend.

6. What would he like to do when he leaves school? – He wants to .... the navy when he's old enough.

7. When she heard the terrible news, she .... tears.

8. The jacket's a bit large but you'll soon .... it.

"Will I ever grow into it?"

2 **Now do the same with these verbs:**

check   crowd   get   let   look   make   pull   put

1. You'll need your confirmation of booking when you .... the hotel.

2. The coach driver .... the car park and the passengers all got out.

3. How do you feel after everything that has happened? – It's difficult to explain. I can't .... it .... words.

4. I never buy anything I can't afford. I don't want to .... debt.

5. Why are the police going around asking people questions? They're .... a robbery at the Town Hall.

6. If you promise not to tell anyone I'll .... you .... a secret.

7. So many people .... the stadium that there was soon no room for any more.

8. What are they going to do with that piece of waste ground? – I've heard that they're going to .... it .... a children's playground.

Notice that the verb in No. 6 has the construction "let ... into". Can you find any more examples of this word order? Remember to keep noticing where the particle comes.

Verbs with INTO – 2

1 **Match a verb on the left with a suitable item on the right. Use each verb and each item once only. Write your answers in the boxes.**

1. dig into   A   the back of a lorry at the traffic lights.

2. fly into   B   his dinner with a great deal of pleasure.

3. lapse into   C   a trap if they aren't careful.

4. get into   D   a rage when she sees all the damage.

5. run into   E   his pocket and pull out a few coins.

6. settle into   F   trouble with the police.

7. tuck into   G   a routine after years of travelling around.

8. walk into   H   the local dialect when speaking to my friends.

"Tucking into his dinner!"

1		2		3		4		5		6		7		8	

2 **Now do the same with these:**

1. fling herself into   A   my leg and refuse to let go.

2. fool them into   B   our confidence because we trust him.

3. see her into   C   an actor by sending him to drama school.

4. sink its teeth into   D   believing they will make a lot of money.

5. shock us into   E   the office and ask her to wait.

6. take him into   F   prison if they cause any more trouble.

7. throw them into   G   silence by showing us those terrible pictures.

8. turn him into   H   her work with such enthusiasm.

1		2		3		4		5		6		7		8	

Test yourself by covering the column on the right and trying to complete the sentence.

Organising Verbs with INTO – 1

Complete each of the groups of sentences with one of the verbs below. Use each verb once only.

burst into	come into	get into	go into
let into	put into	run into	take into

1.

The car had		the back of a bus. It was a write-off.
The cost of rebuilding could		millions of pounds.
They've		difficulties over finance.

2.

They expect to		money when she dies.
The system didn't		use until it had been thoroughly tested.
Why does his colour		it? Surely it's not relevant.

3.

I'm too fat! I can't		these trousers any more!
She won't		college unless she works harder.
If you		difficulties, let me know.

4.

The children		tears when I said they couldn't go.
The engine suddenly		flames while we were driving along.
The audience		loud applause as the curtain came down.

5.

They didn't		any details of the accident.
She's had to		hospital for an operation.
He hopes to		the navy when he's old enough.

6.

I had a key so I was able to	(him)	the house.
We trusted him so we	(him)	our secret.
I don't think we should	(him)	our plan. I don't trust him.

7.

The boss wants to	(her)	the company as a junior partner.
I didn't trust her enough to	(her)	my confidence.
We've called an ambulance to	(her)	hospital.

8.

You need to	(more effort)	your work.
It's difficult to	(my ideas)	words.
Do you think she'll	(more money)	the business?

Organising Verbs with INTO – 2

Complete each definition with a suitable verb from the list below. Use each verb once only.

bump	fly	shock	check	fool
pull	slip	crowd	grow	rush
tune	fling	look	see	walk

1. .... **into**   If you .... someone, you meet them by chance.

2. .... **into**   Things which .... you .... silence are so terrible that you don't know what to say.

3. .... **into**   When you .... a hotel, you arrive, give your details, and take the room key.

4. .... **into**   When you .... someone .... a room, you go with them into the room to make sure they get there.

5. .... **into**   When you .... clothes, you become large enough for them to fit you properly.

6. .... **into**   When the police .... a crime, they investigate it.

7. .... **into**   If you .... someone .... believing something, you make them believe something that is not true.

8. .... **into**   You could .... a trap if you are careless and don't think about possible dangers.

9. .... **into**   Coaches which .... a car park go off the road and into the car park to break a journey.

10. .... **into**   People who .... a place go there in large numbers.

11. .... **into**   If you .... a decision, you decide to do something without taking time to think about it.

12. .... **into**   If you .... a rage, you suddenly become very angry.

13. .... **into**   If you .... someone .... doing something, you persuade them to do it.

14. .... **into**   If you .... a radio station, you set the control on your radio so that you can hear that station clearly.

15. .... **into**   If you .... yourself .... your work, you do it with a lot of energy and enthusiasm.

Test yourself by covering the right-hand column and trying to remember the definition.

Verbs with IN – 1

1 Complete each of the groups of sentences by using the correct form of the verbs given and the particle IN. Use each verb once only.

ask   butt   key   let   lock   look   pour   smash

1. Refugees are still .... and the authorities are running out of food and shelter.

2. I wonder if my prints are ready.
   – I'll .... at the photographer's on the way home and find out.

3. Don't leave your friend on the doorstep! .... him .... !

4. This is an exclusive disco. They won't .... you .... unless you're wearing a tie.

5. We were having a private conversation and he just .... !

6. Because of a shortage of staff, prisoners were .... for most of the day and only let out for meals and an hour's exercise.

7. By using their axes the firemen managed to .... the door and rescue the boy.

8. To start the program the computer operator has to .... a special password.

2 Now do the same with these verbs:

drop   fall   fit   join   pay   push   send   stay

1. There's something good on television so I think I'll .... tonight.

2. Amy used to .... on her way home to tell us what she'd been doing.

3. We were invited to a karaoke evening but I was too embarrassed to .... the singing!

4. When Jenkins finally arrives, I want you to .... him .... immediately!

5. We need a bigger car. All this luggage won't .... !

6. Four people were injured when the ceiling .... and they were trapped under it.

7. The treasurer went to the bank to .... the money they'd collected.

8. The people in the queue got very angry when she tried to ....

"I have a feeling it's not going to fit in."

Did you notice that the verbs in this exercise had the meaning of an inward movement, of being inside, or of being involved or included in an activity? Can you think of any more verbs with IN with these meanings?

Verbs with IN – 2

1   **Match one half of the dialogue on the left with the other half on the right.
Write your answers in the boxes.**

1. Why have you come home from the beach early?

2. I didn't have time to finish my homework last night.

3. They still haven't reached an agreement after all this time.

4. Why doesn't this toaster work?

5. Did you have to leave that man standing outside in the cold?

6. Mr Wood has arrived.

7. I've had enough. I just can't go any further.

8. What kind of response have you had to your appeal for information?

A   I couldn't invite him in. The house was in a terrible mess.

B   It's been fantastic! Letters have come flooding in.

C   I know you're tired but don't give in now. We're nearly there.

D   Show him in straightaway, please.

E   It looks as if I'll have to step in and try and force them to agree.

F   It helps if you plug it in first!

G   The sun went in and it got cold.

H   Well, make sure you hand it in by tomorrow afternoon at the latest!

1		2		3		4		5		6		7		8	

2   **Now do the same with these dialogues:**

1. We've got a busy day ahead of us tomorrow.

2. Why are you so late? School finished ages ago!

3. We've been driving for hours and I'm starving!

4. Wasn't the language in that programme appalling!

5. Have all the miners been rescued?

6. How does Gemma feel about winning first prize?

7. These changes could cause a lot of trouble.

8. Let's go and wish Mrs Monks a happy birthday.

A   I'm afraid not. There are still some missing after the roof caved in.

B   It's hard to say. I don't think the news has really sunk in yet.

C   That's why I want to phase them in gradually.

D   OK. I'll pull in at the next service station and we can have a bite to eat.

E   But it's a private party! You can't just barge in without an invitation!

F   The teacher kept us in until we'd finished our work.

G   Yes, we ought to write in and complain.

H   We'd better turn in early and get a good night's sleep, then.

1		2		3		4		5		6		7		8	

Now underline all the phrasal verbs.

Verbs with IN – 3

1 **Complete each of the groups of sentences by using the correct form of the verbs given and the particle IN. Use each verb once only.**

break   bring   call   come   fill   get   put   take

1. Tourism .... over five million pounds every year.

2. Keep that old brush. It might .... useful one day.

3. My sister finally .... from work at 10 o'clock last night.

4. We couldn't mend the burst pipe so we had to .... a plumber.

5. Could I just .... for a moment to find out how many of you would like coffee?

6. As you don't know what's been going on, I'd better .... you ....

7. The salesman's story sounded so convincing that we were completely ....

8. The staff .... a request for more money but it was turned down.

2 **Now use the same verbs in these sentences:**

1. Once I've .... the shower, the bathroom will be ready.

2. The thieves ...., but the only thing they took was the video.

3. News has just .... that another survivor has been found.

4. Everyone expected the jury to .... a verdict of "not guilty".

5. I'll .... on the way to town and see if there's any shopping she wants me to get.

6. Please make sure you .... the application form correctly.

7. The old woman had nowhere to sleep so we decided to .... her .... for the night.

8. The train leaves Perth at 6 and .... at 7.30.

'Make sure you fill it in in capital letters.'

Organising Verbs with IN – 1

Complete each of the groups of sentences with one of the verbs. Use each verb once only.

	break in	**call in**	**fill in**	**put in**
	bring in	**come in**	**get in**	**take in**

1.	What time does she		from work?
	The team must		some more practice.
	We must		all that washing before it rains.

2.	I'll		and see her on the way home.
	I'm afraid we need to		an expert.
	The company has had to		all the cars to check them.

3.	We expect the jury to		a verdict of "not guilty".
	The police decided to		all the suspects.
	This job can		over six hundred pounds a week.

4.	The thieves tried to		and steal the jewels.
	Excuse me, can I		here and make a suggestion?
	I'm sorry to		but there's an important call on the line.

5.	It was difficult to		everything she said.
	The conman managed to		almost everybody.
	Now I'm slimmer, I must		these trousers.

6.	They've		a request for more equipment.
	It's warmer since we		central heating.
	Some employees		over fifty hours a week.

7.	Could you		this form, please.
	We can		the details later.
	Her deputy had to		for her when she was ill.

8.	This brush might		useful.
	We didn't expect her to		first.
	I'll wait for the tide to		before going swimming.

Can you think of any more expressions using these verbs?

Organising Verbs with IN – 2

Complete each of the groups of sentences with one of the verbs below. Use each verb once only.

fit in	**go in**	**pull in**	**turn in**
give in	**let in**	**send in**	**write in**

1.

Could you		your form as soon as possible, please?
I've decided to		for more information.
They'll have to		the army if the rioting continues.

2.

I think I'll		early tonight. I'm so tired.
My students always		work of a very high standard.

3.

Championship matches usually		a large crowd.
Shall we		at that restaurant over there?
He saw the train		but no passengers got off.

4.

He's in hospital. He had to		for a minor operation.
They watched the sun		behind a cloud.
This stuff will never all		The case is far too small.

5.

I don't really		with the rest of the group.
How does she manage to		all the work? She's so busy.
The hall's full. We can't		any more chairs.

6.

My foot is wet! This shoe must		water.
The doorman only		people who were wearing smart clothes.
Without a ticket I was		by a side door.

7.

Keep going! Don't		now! You've nearly finished!
Please		your homework by Friday morning.
I have always said I'd never		to pressure. So the answer is still no!

8.

We want viewers to		with their ideas for new programmes.
You forgot to		some of the details on this form.
The competition asks you to		with a slogan of your own.

Test yourself by covering the phrasal verbs.

Organising Verbs with IN – 3

Complete each definition below using a verb from the list below. Use each verb once only.

barge in	join in	plug in	sink in
drop in	key in	pour in	smash in
hand in	pay in	push in	stay in
invite in	phase in	show in	step in

1. .... **in** — People who .... rush rudely into a place or interrupt a conversation that is nothing to do with them.

2. .... **in** — People who .... when there is a queue, get into the queue in front of other people.

3. .... **in** — When you .... information, you type it into a computer.

4. .... **in** — When refugees ...., they enter a country in large numbers.

5. .... **in** — If there is an argument and you ...., you become involved and try to get people to reach an agreement.

6. .... **in** — When you .... some work you've done, you give it to someone.

7. .... **in** — If you .... someone ...., you ask them to come into your home.

8. .... **in** — If you .... someone ...., you go with them into a room.

9. .... **in** — When an activity is taking place and you ...., you do that activity with the other people.

10. .... **in** — If you ...., you visit someone without telling them you are coming.

11. .... **in** — When you .... changes, you introduce them gradually.

12. .... **in** — When you .... a machine, you connect it to a supply of electricity.

13. .... **in** — If you .... a door..........., you hit it violently until it falls into pieces.

14. .... **in** — When news begins to ...., a person begins to realise the importance of what has happened.

15. .... **in** — When you ...., you decide not to go out.

16. .... **in** — When you .... money, you put the money into a bank account.

Test yourself by covering the right-hand column and trying to remember the definitions.

Verbs with ON – 1

1 **Complete each sentence with the correct form of one of the verbs given and the particle ON. Use each verb once only.**

bring   count   drag   hit   look   stay   switch   wave

1. .... the kettle ....! Let's have a cup of tea!

2. The spectators .... helplessly as the car burst into flames.

3. Ivy left school at sixteen but her friend .... to get better qualifications.

4. At the road block the police .... us .... but the car behind had to stop.

5. I'll help you all I can. You can .... my full support.

6. While we were talking we .... an idea for making extra money.

7. All the excitement .... an asthma attack so we tried to calm him down.

8. Some people got very restless as the meeting .... past 10 o'clock..

2 **Now do the same with these verbs:**

add   carry   hold   live
send   sew   touch   try

1. You can write to my parents' house. They'll .... any letters to my new address.

2. I'm not sure if this dress is my size. Can I .... it ....?

3. A button has come off my jacket.
   – And I suppose you'd like me to .... it ..... again!

4. Could you .... a moment? This won't take long.

5. That's not the total cost. You have to .... ten to fifteen per cent for postage and packing.

6. My wife has to go out to work as we can't .... my wages alone.

7. The dog's owner took no notice of our protests but .... hitting the poor defenceless animal.

8. During my talk I'll try to .... some of the problems that have come up in the last few months.

" I just carried on doodling as the meeting dragged on and on and on."

Verbs with ON – 2

1   Match one half of the dialogue on the left with the other half on the right. Write your answers in the boxes.

1. What do you think of this new dance?

2. You can't see much of the valley from here.

3. Could you tell him that his mother will be there at six?

4. Why didn't Mary tell me they'd planned a party for me?

5. Shall I switch the TV off?

6. Lots of people want to go on the excursion.

7. Do you know how badly people were injured in the accident?

8. How many people do you think will come to the meeting?

A   She didn't want to let on and spoil the surprise.

B   No I don't. The police moved us on so I didn't see very much.

C   In that case we'll have to lay on some extra coaches.

D   It's a bit strange. I don't think it'll catch on.

E   You can reckon on at least fifty.

F   Let's walk on a bit and see if we can get a better view somewhere else.

G   No problem. I'll pass on the message when I see him this afternoon.

H   Could you leave it on? I want to watch the news.

1		2		3		4		5		6		7		8	

2   Now do the same with these dialogues:

1. You'd better wear a hat.

2. Cars cause so much damage!

3. So you caught the train after all.

4. When did you realise you'd been tricked?

5. What's your company's latest project?

6. Bill's looking really tired and worried these days.

7. I hate it when Ted chairs the meeting.

8. What's the attitude of your staff towards you?

A   At least mine runs on unleaded petrol.

B   Yes, he just rambles on and on and on!

C   Yes, he is. The strain of not finding a job is beginning to tell on him.

D   We're working on a new type of fuel.

E   I suppose they look on me as a kind of father figure.

F   It didn't dawn on me till much later.

G   Yes. I just managed to jump on as it was leaving the station.

H   Don't be silly. It'll never stay on in this wind.

"It'll never stay on!."

1		2		3		4		5		6		7		8	

Verbs with ON – 3

1 **Complete each sentence with the correct form of one of the verbs given and the particle ON. Use each verb once only.**

call   come   get   go   keep   put   take   turn

1. We haven't got much information to ...., but we'll do our best.

2. There's a terrific atmosphere at work. All the staff .... really well.

3. I wish Mr Thomas wouldn't .... criticising me all the time.

4. The dog hadn't been at all agressive so I didn't expect it to .... me and attack me like that.

5. Do you have to .... special make-up when you appear on television?

6. In his speech the boss said that he needed everyone's help. He .... all his employees to do their best to increase sales.

7. When exactly do you get these headaches?
   – They usually seem to .... in the evening.

8. I need a break. I realise now that I've .... too much work.

2 **Now use the same verbs with these sentences:**

1. Don't stop. Please .... and tell us what happened next.

2. One of their salesmen .... me yesterday but I told him I wasn't really interested.

3. It was a terrible film!
   – Oh, ... ! It wasn't that bad!

4. The plane landed at Frankfurt to .... more passengers.

5. How old is your uncle?
   – He's .... a bit now. He must be at least eighty.

6. I ate too much during my holiday and .... quite a lot of weight.

7. I'm afraid I can't .... you all .... – there just isn't enough work!

8. .... the hot water, will you? I think I'll have a bath.

"I suppose I HAVE put on a little weight."

Have you noticed that all the pictures include a phrasal verb? Go through the book and underline the phrasal verbs below the pictures.

Organising Verbs with ON – 1

Complete each of the groups of sentences with one of the phrasal verbs below. Use each verb once only.

call on	**get on**	**keep on**	**take on**
come on	**go on**	**put on**	**turn on**

1.
Do these headaches		at any particular time?
When do the street lights		at night?
The star doesn't		until halfway through the play.

2.
The bus stopped to		more passengers.
We've had to		more staff to meet the demand.
Why did he		all that extra work?

3.
Could you		her on your way home?
I		everyone to do their best.
I'd like to		Lady Porter to propose a vote of thanks.

4.
She can certainly		the charm.
Why would the dog		her like that?
I heard him		the shower.

5.
Oh dear! I've		more than 3 kilos over Christmas.
The scouts are going to		a show.
Why does he have to		that silly accent!

6.
I think I		well with most people.
Well, I must		I've got work to do.
As you		you pay the driver.

7.
Does this kind of thing		in your country?
More money will		clothes as they get older.
She fixed the light to		automatically.

8.
Why do you		phoning her all the time?
I wish I could		all the staff.
I don't know why I		working. I AM 75!

Test yourself by covering the phrasal verbs.

Organising Verbs with ON – 2

Complete each of the groups of sentences by using one of the phrasal verbs below. Use each verb once only.

bring on	live on	move on	stay on
catch on	look on	pass on	work on

1.

Shall we		and discuss something else?
The police tried to		the people near the scene of the accident.
One day I hope to		to a job with more responsibility.

2.

Can't you		her and get her to change her mind?
Students need to		their vocabulary every day.
We need to		providing a better service.

3.

How can she manage to		such a low salary?
His reputation will		long after he has retired.
I don't want to		fruit and salad. I actually like meat!

4.

The new fashion didn't		as the journalists had predicted.
When did she finally		and realise it was all a joke?
Once you		it's quite easy to understand.

5.

Too much excitement could		a heart attack.
We must improve the team and		any promising athletes.
I hope this warm weather doesn't		my hay fever.

6.

My hat wouldn't		in the wind.
I've decided to		at school to get more qualifications.
The lights often		all night in some of the offices.

7.

I want you to		me as a friend.
She could only		in horror as the fire spread.
Please come, my boss will		it as my fault if you don't.

8.

Don't worry. I'll		the message when I see her.
I'm afraid it's very easy to		this disease.
We'll have to		most of the cost to our customers.

Test yourself by covering the phrasal verbs.

Organising Verbs with ON – 3

Complete the definitions using the phrasal verbs below. Use each verb once only.

carry on	hold on	ramble on	tell on
count on	lay on	run on	touch on
drag on	leave on	send on	try on
hit on	let on	switch on	wave on

1. .... **on**   People who .... keep talking for a long time in a very disorganised way.

2. .... **on**   Meetings that .... continue unneccessarily for a long time.

3. .... **on**   If people are trying to keep something secret and you ...., you tell somebody that secret.

4. .... **on**   If you .... doing something, you continue doing it.

5. .... **on**   People you can .... will support and help you as they have promised.

6. .... **on**   If you .... some kind of service, you provide that service.

7. .... **on**   If you ask someone to ...., you want them to wait.

8. .... **on**   Cars that .... unleaded petrol are more environmentally friendly.

9. .... **on**   If you .... an idea, you suddenly think of it.

10. .... **on**   If you .... a letter, you send it to a person's new address.

11. .... **on**   When you .... electrical equipment, you start it working.

12. .... **on**   If you .... the television ...., you don't switch it off.

13. .... **on**   If you .... a subject while you are speaking, you mention it briefly.

14. .... **on**   When you .... an item of clothing, you put it on to see if it fits.

15. .... **on**   When the police .... a car, they signal it to continue and not stop.

16. .... **on**   If some kind of pressure is beginning to .... you, you are showing signs of being affected by that pressure.

Test yourself by covering the right-hand column.

Verbs with OFF – 1

1 **Complete each sentence with the correct form of one of the verbs given and the particle OFF. Use each verb once only.**

> **break   cordon   cut   make   scare   show   switch   tell**

1. Save electricity. Please .... any unnecessary lights.

2. We were chatting on the phone when we were suddenly ....

3. Our neighbour bought an enormous guard dog and had outside lighting installed to .... burglars.

4. My ex-girlfriend was the one who .... our relationship, not me!

5. When Yvette came home late, her mother was very angry and .... her ....

6. Keith's always talking about his latest car to .... but nobody is impressed.

"Told off! Again!"

7. The thieves attacked her and .... down the road, taking the money with them.

8. There's been a bomb scare and the police have .... the area.

2 **Now do the same with these verbs:**

> **clear   fight   laugh   pull   round   see   work   write**

1. I saw the advertisement and decided to .... for further details.

2. I wish you'd .... ! I don't want to speak to you!

3. Agnes tried to .... the accident but you could see she was really upset by what had happened.

4. My mother used to send me out to run round the park and .... some of my energy.

5. Finally, to .... the evening, there'll be a disco.

6. The old man used his stick to try and .... the mugger.

7. I don't know how she managed to .... it .... but she succeeded in making her boss change his mind.

8. As my sister was going to be away for a long time, we all went to the station to .... her.......... .

Verbs with OFF – 2

1 **Match an item on the left with an item on the right. Use each item once only. Write your answers in the boxes.**

1. A button
2. The caller
3. The chauffeur
4. The pain
5. The news
6. The rain
7. The rocket
8. The sleepy children

A dozed off because they'd had such a tiring day.
B drove off in his employer's Rolls Royce.
C fell off and rolled under the chair.
D sparked off a violent demonstration.
E held off and we were able to have our picnic.
F lifted off and soon disappeared in the clouds.
G rang off without leaving his phone number.
H wore off after the doctor gave her an injection.

1		2		3		4		5		6		7		8	

2 **Now do the same with these:**

1. call off
2. fence off
3. keep off
4. give off
5. live off
6. scrape off
7. send off
8. shave off

A this area to stop people getting in.
B his beard as his new girlfriend doesn't like it.
C a letter asking for more information.
D the meeting as so many people are away.
E the State.
F the paint with a knife.
G a strange smell which makes me feel ill.
H the subject as she's still very upset about it all.

"I'm only shaving it off because I love her!"

1		2		3		4		5		6		7		8	

Test yourself by covering one column and trying to remember the other part.

Verbs with OFF – 3

1 **Complete each sentence with the correct form of one of the verbs given and the particle OFF. Use each verb once only.**

come get go let put set take turn

1. Some people aren't here today so we've decided to .... the meeting .... until next week.

2. .... the bus at Beecher Road and take the first on the left.

3. All the posters had .... so I had to stick them up again.

4. There's a long journey ahead of us so we want to .... early.

5. There was a bomb scare and the plane .... an hour late.

6. Suddenly the alarm .... and the guards rushed in.

7. Don't forget to .... the electric fire before you go to bed.

8. I asked the driver to .... me .... at the end of my road.

2 **Now use the same verbs with these sentences:**

1. You have to .... the main road by the pub and go down a narrow lane until you get to a farm.

2. I think this yoghurt has .... It smells strange.

3. Only two months in prison! He .... very lightly!

4. You'd better .... those wet clothes and have a bath.

5. If he ever does it again he'll be severely punished, but I'll .... him .... this time.

6. I was trying to concentrate but the noise kept .... me ....

7. England played very well.
   – .... it! They still lost!

8. Be careful not to .... the burglar alarm by accident. It makes a terrible noise!

"It HAS gone off, hasn't it!"

Organising Verbs with OFF – 1

Complete each of the groups of sentences with one of the phrasal verbs below. Use each verb once only.

come off	**go off**	**put off**	**take off**
get off	**let off**	**set off**	**turn off**

1.

You have to		at the next stop.
He'll probably		with just a fine.
I didn't		to sleep until very late.

2.

Don't be		by the noise – if will soon get quieter.
Don't forget to		the lights when you go.
The meeting has been		until Friday.

3.

The players had to		because it was raining.
The label must have		in the post.
He should		best in the competition.

4.

The cheese will		unless you eat it soon.
What made the alarm		just now?
You can		people, you know!

5.

The plane is due to		in a few minutes.
You can		your jacket if you like.
We always		ten per cent for regular orders.

6.

You have to		this road in a minute.
Can you		that racket! I can't hear myself think!
Why don't you		the engine? We'll be stuck here for an hour.

7.

The thief must have		the alarm.
The travellers		early in the morning.
You press this to		the explosives.

8.

The coach driver	(her)	at the end of the road.
The judge	(her)	with just a fine.
Will the teacher	(her)	doing her homework?

Test yourself by covering the phrasal verbs.

Organising Verbs with OFF – 2

Complete each of the groups of sentences with one of the phrasal verbs below. Use each verb once only.

break off	fall off	pull off	show off
cut off	keep off	send off	switch off

1.

Why did he		their relationship?
Shall I		a piece of chocolate and give it to him?
We usually		for coffee halfway through the meeting.

2.

Let's		the road for a while and have a rest.
Can you help me to		my boots?
How did he manage to		such an important deal?

3.

You'd better		the subject of boyfriends for a while!
Please		the grass.
Do you think the rain will		all day?

4.

The town was		by an avalanche.
We were		in the middle of our phone conversation.
He		a small piece for me to taste.

5.

He might		if he walks along the top of the wall.
Business began to		and some employees lost their jobs.
Student numbers started to		when the fees went up.

6.

Why don't you		for more information?
Referees should		any players that cause trouble.
I must remember to		my application today.

7.

Don't		like that. Nobody's impressed.
He couldn't wait to		his new bicycle.
People who		, clearly have problems.

8.

Don't forget to		the television before you go out.
I tend to		when he speaks. He's so boring.
I always		the electricity before going on holiday.

Test yourself by covering the phrasal verbs.

Organising Verbs with OFF – 3

Complete the definitions using the verbs below. Use each verb once only.

call	fight	lift	see	cordon
live	tell	doze	hold	make
wear	drive	laugh	scrape	work

1. .... **off**   If you .... excess energy, you do something active to get rid of it.

2. .... **off**   If the police .... an area, they erect barriers around it to restrict movement.

3. .... **off**   If you .... someone ...., you tell them you strongly disapprove of something they have done.

4. .... **off**   If you .... a wild dog, you try to stop it coming near and attacking you.

5. .... **off**   When rockets ...., they rise into the air.

6. .... **off**   When you ...., you leave a place in some kind of vehicle.

7. .... **off**   If you try to .... something that has happened, you pretend it was not at all important.

8. .... **off**   Thieves who .... with your money escape with it.

9. .... **off**   If showers of rain ...., they come later than expected or maybe not at all.

10. .... **off**   If you .... a meeting, you cancel it.

11. .... **off**   When pains ...., they stop hurting you.

12. .... **off**   When you .... someone ...., you say goodbye to them before they start a journey.

13. .... **off**   If you .... the State, it gives you the money you need to support yourself.

14. .... **off**   If you .... some paint from a surface, you use a knife or something similar to remove it.

15. .... **off**   If you ...., you fall into a light sleep without intending to because you are very tired.

Test yourself by covering one of the columns.

Unit 47

Verbs with ABOUT, ACROSS, AFTER and BY

1 **Complete each sentence with the correct form of one of the verbs given. Use each verb once only.**

bring about	**get by**	**go by**	**stand by**
come across	**go after**	**set about**	**take after**

1. If you're in trouble, Tommy's the kind of friend who will .... you.

2. I just can't find a job anywhere.
   – Why don't you .... that vacancy at the sports centre?

3. The victims of the accident gradually got better as the days ....

4. Your son is clever, isn't he?
   – Yes, he .... his mother!

5. I was sorting through some papers when I .... these old photos.

6. The counsellor is trying to .... a reconciliation between the two of them.

7. By cutting out luxuries we manage to .... on just one salary.

8. This booklet gives tips on how to .... losing weight.

"He takes after his mother."

2 **Now do the same with these sentences:**

call after	**get across**	**go about**	**put by**
come across	**get by**	**look after**	**stand by**

1. I've been saving part of my wages each week so I've got some money .... in case of emergencies.

2. We decided to .... the baby `Ian' .... his grandfather.

3. There's a spare bus .... in case too many people turn up.

4. At night there are only three nurses to .... all the patients in this ward.

5. As I only had a short time to explain things to the audience, it was very difficult to .... my message ....

6. You're blocking the corridor! Stand to one side so that people can ....

7. The new manageress .... as a really nice person, doesn't she?

8. I'm sure there's a much easier way to tackle this problem. I think I've been .... it the wrong way.

58

Verbs with AWAY

1 **Match an item on the left with an item on the right. Use each item once only. Write your answers in the boxes.**

1. The fire

2. The noise

3. My grandfather

4. The police

5. Support for him

6. The little girl

7. The thieves

8. The wood

A backed away as the huge dog came towards her.

B blazed away and we soon got warm again.

C died away as the audience settled down.

D dropped away as people began to doubt his ability.

E scared away the hooligans before they did any damage.

F got away in a car they had stolen.

G rotted away and we had to buy a new door.

H passed away quietly in his sleep.

1		2		3		4		5		6		7		8	

2 **Now do the same with these:**

1. clear away

2. file away

3. gamble away

4. give away

5. pour away

6. sign away

7. turn away

8. while away

A customers because we've sold out.

B the dishes from the dinner table.

C all her money at the casino.

D this report with the others.

E the time, sitting in the garden.

F the secret.

G the tea as it's got cold.

H your rights to your share of the estate.

"She's gambled away a fortune."

1		2		3		4		5		6		7		8	

Test yourself by covering one column and trying to remember the other part.

Verbs with AGAINST, APART, AROUND and BACK

1 **Complete each sentence with the correct form of one of the verbs given. Use each verb once only.**

get around	**hold against**	**ring back**	**take apart**
get back	**look around**	**shop around**	**take back**

1. The news of their engagement will soon ....

2. We spent the afternoon .... an old castle.

3. You might be able to buy the camera at a lower price if you ....

4. After climbing the hill, we stopped for a moment to .... our breath ....

5. I know Danny made a mess of things but don't .... it .... him. He was only trying to help.

6. I had no difficulty .... the engine .... Putting it back together again was a problem, though.

7. If you give me your number, I'll .... you .... when I get more news.

8. I've changed my mind. Simon's quite nice, really. I .... what I said.

2 **Now do the same with these verbs:**

come apart	**fall back**	**hang around**	**turn against**
crowd around	**give back**	**tell apart**	**turn back**

1. The attack was so fierce that the soldiers had to ....

2. His wife was the only one who supported him. All his friends had .... him.

3. When they wear the same clothes, it's hard to .... the twins ....

4. The road was blocked so we .... and looked for another route.

5. Look at those kids! Can't they think of something better to do than just .... smoking.

6. My neighbour has finally .... the tools he borrowed!

"Can you tell them apart?"

7. We tried to speak to the Prime Minister but everyone had .... him so we couldn't get anywhere near him.

8. I'm sorry I broke your pen, but it just .... in my hands.

Verbs with OVER and THROUGH

1 **Match an item on the left with an item on the right. Use each item once only. Write your answers in the boxes.**

1.	The car	A	blew over and the sun came out.
2.	His eyes	B	boiled over and went all over the stove.
3.	The milk	C	came through so I was able to go to Australia.
4.	The plan	D	clouded over and it looked as if it was going to rain.
5.	The sky	E	fell through and we had to start again.
6.	The storm	F	glazed over and he fell back into the armchair.
7.	My visa finally	G	healed over and she didn't need a plaster any more.
8.	The wound	H	pulled over and the driver asked for directions.

1		2		3		4		5		6		7		8	

2 **Now do the same with these:**

1.	break through	A	the barrier and try to reach the President.
2.	go through	B	his disguise and contact the police.
3.	get over	C	an old lady crossing the road.
4.	hand over	D	my notes to refresh my memory.
5.	run over	E	that phone call to the boss's secretary.
6.	put through	F	a terrifying ordeal that they'll never forget.
7.	see through	G	responsibility to someone with better training.
8.	sleep through	H	the thunderstorm while everyone was woken up.

"Run over while crossing the road."

1		2		3		4		5		6		7		8	

Test yourself by covering one of the columns.

Verbs with WITH

1   **Complete each sentence with the correct form of one of the verbs given and the particle WITH. Use each verb once only.**

deal   do   fill   go   lie   part   play   reason

1. If there are any complaints, the manager will .... them.

2. Shall I get those blue curtains?
    – No. They don't really .... the carpet. You need a lighter colour.

3. Once Jonathon's got an idea into his head, he won't change his mind. I tried to .... him but it was no use.

4. Julia wanted to sell their car but her husband was reluctant to .... it.

5. I'm really thirsty. I could .... a long cool drink.

6. That woman from head office talks about `participation' and `consultation' but it doesn't mean anything. She's just .... words.

7. The way he drives all over the road doesn't exactly .... me .... confidence!

8. Who do you think is to blame for the accident?
    – In my opinion the fault .... the council for not taking better precautions.

2   **Now do the same with these verbs:**

confuse   deal   disagree   identify   live   meet   side   wrestle

1. It's my decision and whatever happens I'll have to .... the consequences.

2. This little booklet .... the problems of living abroad.

3. While Louise was on her way to the meeting, she .... an accident and had to be taken to hospital.

4. And you're an engineer, aren't you?
    – No. I'm in marketing. I think you're .... me .... my brother.

5. I've decided to resign. I've spent the last twenty years .... the financial problems of this company and I've had enough of it!

6. We want the play to be as realistic as possible. The main character, for example, must be somebody the audience can easily ....

7. Whenever there was a family dispute, her son agreed with her while her daughters used to .... her husband.

8. I try never to eat anything with onion in as it always .... me.

Verbs with AT and TO

1 **Match one half of the dialogue on the left with the other half on the right. Write your answers in the boxes.**

1. My car wouldn't start this morning.

2. Why doesn't Ted want to play with the other children?

3. I think that new magazine is very childish!

4. Would Blake be interested in making some extra money?

5. I hear you're going to New Zealand.

6. Did the police manage to get anyone to talk about the fight?

7. Were they very hungry?

8. This maths homework is driving me crazy!

A No they weren't. They just picked at their food and ate hardly anything

B No, they didn't. It's going to be very difficult to get at the truth.

C Yes, I was offered a job there – so I leapt at the opportunity to work 'Down Under'.

D He's afraid they'll laugh at his accent.

E You'd better get the garage to look at it, then.

F I know it's hard, but you must keep at it. Don't give up now!

G I'm sure he'd jump at the chance.

H Well, it's not really for adults. It's aimed more at the teenage market.

1		2		3		4		5		6		7		8	

2 **Now do the same with these dialogues:**

1. I think this is your coat.

2. Why didn't you offer to help them prepare dinner?

3. How long was Ben unconscious?

4. Shall I pour?

5. Those customers have been waiting for ages!

6. It's so difficult to get a clear answer from him!

7. Why does Ann keep criticising me all the time?

8. And Judy here is in the final tomorrow.

A Thanks - and help yourself to sugar.

B I know! He keeps getting side-tracked. I wish he'd stick to the point.

C Well, let's drink to her success, then.

D No. That one belongs to Mike. Mine's grey.

E Don't let it get to you. She does it to everyone. Just ignore her.

F Because when it comes to cooking, I'm totally useless.

G Could you see to them? I'm really busy at the moment.

H It took him at least a quarter of an hour to come to.

1		2		3		4		5		6		7		8	

Now go through the sentences on the right and underline the phrasal verbs.

Verbs with FOR

1 **Complete each sentence with the correct form of one of the verbs given and the particle FOR. Use each verb once only.**

> **ask   call   enter   go   look   make   send   stand**

1. She's been .... a job for ages and she still hasn't found one.

2. So you've passed your exam. This .... a celebration!

3. He hasn't decided which to buy but he'll probably .... the flat in the city centre.

4. They were so hungry after their day out that they .... the nearest restaurant.

5. If the fever continues, I'll have to .... the doctor.

6. If I were you, I wouldn't mention her driving test. You'd be .... trouble!

7. I never dreamt I'd win when I .... the competition!

8. What do the initials BBC .... ?

2 **Now do the same with these verbs:**

> **account   call   fall   fish   go   hope   mistake   pay**

1. I just hope you've got enough money with you to .... all this food!

2. The dog .... his ankle and gave him a nasty bite.

3. People often .... me .... my sister. We've got the same hair.

4. I'd better start getting ready. He's going to .... me at six.

5. You could see she was .... compliments by the way she kept talking about her dress.

6. How do you .... his reaction?
   – I couldn't understand it.

"Here was I minding my own business when it went for my ankle!"

7. I'd like you to tidy your room or is that too much to .... ?

8. How could I have .... such an obvious trick? I'm not usually taken in like that.

64

Verbs with FROM and OF

1 **Match the first part of the dialogue on the left with the second part on the right. Write your answers in the boxes.**

1. Why are you back living with your parents again?

2. What's this new exercise video you've bought?

3. Any news of your sister?

4. I'm leaving! I can't work under these conditions any longer!

5. You're French, aren't you?

6. I hope Mum doesn't find out I've been seeing Nigel.

7. I'm off to the beach, then.

8. Why has Phil been off work for so long?

A   Take this hat with you. It'll protect you from the sun.

B   Fine, but don't resign from this job until you've got another one to go to.

C   No. I come from Belgium.

D   I was behind with the rent so I was evicted from my flat.

E   Yes. I finally heard from her last week.

F   The exercises on it are for people who suffer from backache.

G   He's still recovering from the accident.

H   But your brother knows, and it'll be hard to keep him from telling her.

1		2		3		4		5		6		7		8	

2 **Now do the same with these dialogues:**

1. Do you think your parents would lend you the money?

2. Are there any jobs going at the hotel?

3. Do you like the new uniform?

4. Shall I make that vegetable soup again?

5. Why were you two boys fighting?

6. Look at the snow on those hills.

7. What are they going to do with all the factory waste?

8. Did you see the look on her father's face?

A   Please don't. The whole house smelt of cabbage last time you made it.

B   I certainly did! He obviously didn't approve of that dress!

C   He started it. He accused me of being a liar so I hit him.

D   They want to dispose of it by dumping it in the sea.

E   It reminds me of the time we went skiing in the Alps.

F   Not at the moment. I'll let you know if I hear of any vacancies.

G   Forget it. I wouldn't dream of asking them for a loan.

H   Well, the style's all right but I don't think much of the colour.

1		2		3		4		5		6		7		8	

Now underline the phrasal verbs.

Organising Verbs with Other Particles – 1

Complete each of the groups of sentences with one of the verbs below. Use each verb once only.

call for	get back	give away	run over
fall for	get over	go through	stand by

1.

I think we should		free samples of the new detergent.
He's offered to		the secrets of his success.
It was wonderful of her to		some of the prize money to charity.

2.

Ask the police to		in case we need them.
A friend will always		you if you're in trouble.
I haven't changed. I		everything I said.

3.

You'd better		your notes again before the speech.
She had to		a terrible ordeal.
The reforms should		without any problems.

4.

Shall I		you on the way to work?
We intend to		an inquiry into the incident.
Such hostile questions		firm answers.

5.

They'll never		their son's death.
It took him a long time to		his operation.
It's a difficult message to		to an audience.

6.

That lorry has just		a cat that ran into the road.
Can we just		the procedure one more time?
Could you		to the post office and get me a stamp?

7.

We didn't		from our holiday until Sunday evening.
She's still waiting to		all the tools she lent them.
I wish they'd		out of the way of the procession.

8.

How could I		such an obvious trick?
She tends to		the most unsuitable men.
You didn't think I'd		that story, did you?

Test yourself by covering the phrasal verbs.

Organising Verbs with Other Particles – 2

Complete each group of sentences with one of the verbs below. Use each verb once only.

| come across | get at | go by | stand for |
| deal with | get by | go for | take back |

1.

We just about managed to		on my salary.
We were able to		with the Spanish we'd learnt at school.
People can't		so please stand back.

2.

As the days		she'll slowly get better.
Don't		that clock. It's slow.
We watched the procession		and head towards the river.

3.

Be careful! He won't		any argument!
What do the initials MA		after his name?
I'm against everything they		! How can I be friends with them?

4.

I'm very busy. Could you		these enquiries, please.
He thinks the magazine should		more controversial topics.
They're a very good firm to		– quick and reliable.

5.

It's going to be hard to		the truth.
Keep your torch where you can		it quickly if you need it.
He's always trying to		me. Why doesn't he like me?

6.

I think they'll		the first option.
Why did the dog		my leg like that?
She doesn't usually		men unless they're well-off.

7.

It's amazing what you		when you tidy a cupboard!
He didn't		as a very pleasant person.
Her ideas don't		very well in her new novel.

8.

Don't forget to		the books you borrowed from the library.
Yes. He's OK. I		all the things I said about him.
These photos	(me)	to when I was a teenager.

Test yourself by covering the phrasal verbs.

Organising Verbs with Other Particles – 3

Complete the definitions with the verbs below. Use each verb once only.

back away	**fall through**	**make for**	**set about**
blow over	**get away**	**pull over**	**take after**
call after	**go after**	**put by**	**while away**
do with	**hand over**	**see through**	**wrestle with**

1. .... If you .... a place, you go towards it.

2. .... If thieves ...., they escape from a place.

3. .... If you say you could .... something, you would really like it or need it.

4. .... If you .... money ...., you save it.

5. .... If you .... what someone says, you understand the real meaning behind what they say.

6. .... Plans which .... do not succeed.

7. .... If you .... responsibility to someone else, you transfer the responsibility to that person.

8. .... When storms ...., they become less strong and finish.

9. .... If you .... your daughter .... someone, you give her the same name as that person.

10. .... If you ...., you move backwards away from someone or something, often because you are afraid.

11. .... When vehicles .... , they go to the side of the road and stop.

12. .... When you .... doing something, you start doing that activity.

13. .... If you .... your mother or father, you are like them physically or in character.

14. .... If you .... a job, you try to get it.

15. .... If you .... the time, you spend time doing something because you have nothing better to do.

16. .... If you .... a problem, you have a lot of difficulty trying to find the solution to that problem.

Test yourself by covering the right-hand column.

Organising Verbs with Other Particles – 4

Complete each of the definitions with the verbs below. Use each verb once only.

get to	identify with	shop around	come apart	glaze over
jump at	tell apart	come to	hang around	pick at
think of	dream of	hear from	reason with	turn against

1. .... If you .... somebody, you no longer support them.

2. .... If you are unconscious and ...., you become conscious again.

3. .... Things which .... you, make you upset.

4. .... If you .... someone, they write to you or phone you.

5. .... If you .... the chance of doing something, you accept that opportunity with enthusiasm.

6. .... If you wouldn't .... doing something, you have no intention of doing it.

7. .... People who .... go from shop to shop to find the best value.

8. .... If you can .... twins .... you know which one is which.

9. .... If you .... someone, you try to use sensible arguments to persuade them to do something.

10. .... Things which .... collapse into pieces.

11. .... People who .... a place, stay there doing nothing important often because they have nothing better to do.

12. .... If your eyes ...., you have a fixed expression, often showing that you are bored with what is happening.

13. .... If you don't .... much .... something or somebody, you don't have a very high opinion of them.

14. .... If you .... a character in a play, you feel that their situation is similar to your own.

15. .... People who .... their food eat small pieces of it.

Test yourself by covering the right-hand column.

Verbs with Two Particles – 1

1 **Complete each sentence with the correct form of one of the verbs below. Use each verb once only.**

add up to	get away with	move on to	stand in for
catch up with	go ahead with	send away for	watch out for

1. The burglar broke into the house and .... all her jewels.

2. Max's been absent from school for three weeks and missed a lot of work. When he comes back, he'll have to work hard to .... the rest of the class.

3. I think we've discussed that long enough. Can we .... another topic now?

4. This advertisement looks interesting. I think I'll .... further details.

"Watch out for ice!"

5. Be careful! .... ice on the road!

6. When we discussed how much our wedding was going to cost, it .... over two thousand pounds!

7. The boss was away so his assistant had to .... him and make the speech.

8. After a long delay we finally got permission to .... the improvements to the heating system.

2 **Now do the same with these verbs:**

come forward with	fool around with	look back on	miss out on
cut back on	go out with	make off with	walk out on

1. When I .... my childhood, I have some wonderful memories.

2. He rode past on a motorbike, snatched her handbag and .... it down the street.

3. After years of being badly treated, she finally .... her husband and was never seen again.

4. Why is Justin spending so much time getting ready?
   – He's .... his new girlfriend tonight.

5. We believe the fire was started by some children who had been .... matches.

6. If sales continue to fall, we'll have to .... production and some employees may lose their jobs.

7. A witness has .... information about the robbery and has given us a very good description of one of the women.

8. I don't think I'll be able to come to the party.
   – Oh no! You'll .... all the fun!

Verbs with Two Particles – 2

1

First, go through the dialogues and underline all the phrasal verbs with two particles. Next, match the two halves of the dialogue.

1. Should she still be sucking her thumb at her age?

2. Is Emily coming out with us this evening?

3. Ken still hasn't decided whether to come or not.

4. So you like living here, then?

5. They've decided not to invest in the company after all.

6. What did the doctor say about your cough?

7. What time are you leaving tomorrow evening?

8. Peter's doing quite well in the race so far.

A Eleven o'clock at the latest. We've got to check out of the hotel by then.

B But they can't just pull out of an agreement like that!

C She told me to cut down on the number of cigarettes I smoke.

D No. She's got some work to catch up on.

E We certainly do. The house is fine and we get on well with the neighbours.

F Yes he is. He's managing to keep up with the leaders.

G Well I hope he does soon. I'm beginning to run out of patience.

H Oh, don't worry! She'll grow out of it.

1		2		3		4		5		6		7		8	

2

Now do the same with these dialogues:

1. Reg hasn't found any work yet.

2. How did you get her to change her mind?

3. What do you know about the new training scheme?

4. We're going jogging now. Are you coming?

5. I hear that Tom and Sue aren't getting married after all.

6. The children are very quiet – too quiet maybe.

7. Why have we got to set out so early? It's stupid!

8. Do you want me to stop for a while?

A No. I don't really feel up to it today.

B I'm not surprised. I didn't think they'd go through with it.

C Look, don't take it out on me! It's not my fault. I wanted to leave later.

D With difficulty! But we finally brought her round to our point of view.

E Oh dear. I wonder if I could fix him up with a temporary job at the hotel.

F Not very much, I'm afraid. Could you fill me in on some of the details?

G No. It's all right. Don't let me disturb you. Carry on with what you're doing.

H I'm sure they're getting up to something we'd rather not know about!

1		2		3		4		5		6		7		8	

Verbs with Two Particles – 3

1 **Complete each sentence with the correct form of one of the verbs given. Use each verb once only.**

bring in on	**get round to**	**go on about**	**stand up to**
do away with	**go back on**	**look down on**	**take up on**

1. We .... Ray .... his offer and stayed at his country cottage.

2. We need another point of view. Let's .... Julie .... our discussion and see what she thinks.

3. Pete is a real snob!
   – You're telling me! He .... anyone who doesn't have a car.

4. Norman is so boring! I wish he wouldn't .... stamp collecting all the time!

5. Charlie's finally .... asking her out. Why did he take so long?

6. I would probably have run away! I didn't think he had the nerve to .... somebody like that!

7. Everybody's relying on you. You can't .... your promise!

8. Pupils can wear what they like now. The headmaster has .... school uniform.

2 **Now do the same with these verbs:**

break in on	**face up to**	**go in for**	**make up for**
bring out in	**go down with**	**look up to**	**take over from**

1. Eating those strawberries has .... me .... a nasty rash.

2. Mrs Kent's students love her. They .... her as a source of inspiration.

3. Cathy doesn't like you. You've got to .... the fact that you're just not her type.

4. Malcolm can't come, I'm afraid. He's .... the flu.

5. I gave her a present to .... all the trouble I'd caused.

6. When I decided to .... the contest I never thought I'd win.

7. It was very rude of that woman to .... our conversation like that!

8. When I .... the previous manager, I had a lot of problems with the staff.

*"I always go in for beauty contests!
I never thought I'd win!"*

Verbs with Two Particles – 4

1 **Match an item on the left with an item on the right. Use each item once only. Write your answers in the boxes.**

1. come in for   A   college because the work was so difficult.

2. come up to   B   a lot of criticism because of his behaviour.

3. come up with   C   his enemies by spreading lies about them.

4. drop out of   D   expectations despite all the problems we had.

5. get back at   E   head office on my portable phone.

6. get down to   F   a rise because she had more work to do.

7. get through to   G   suggestions for improving our environment.

8. put in for   H   some work after sitting around doing nothing.

1		2		3		4		5		6		7		8	

2 **Now do the same with these sentences:**

1. come up against   A   the armchair and go to sleep.

2. come out in   B   hearing from you as soon as possible.

3. get behind with   C   her reputation as a superb singer.

4. go along with   D   quite a lot of problems.

5. live up to   E   your rights as a citizen.

6. look forward to   F   your work.

7. sink back into   G   the decision although I'm not happy about it.

8. stand up for   H   spots after eating those strawberries.

"Homework brings me out in spots, too!"

1		2		3		4		5		6		7		8	

Test yourself by covering the right-hand column and trying to complete the sentences.

Organising Verbs with Two Particles – 1

Complete the definitions with the verbs below. Use each verb once only.

break in on	**cut back on**	**get on with**	**look back on**
carry on with	**feel up to**	**get round to**	**look forward to**
come forward with	**fill (someone) in on**	**get through to**	**stand in for**
come in for	**fool around with**	**go down with**	**take over from**

1. .... If you .... people, you have a good relationship with them.

2. .... If you don't .... something, you don't feel well enough to do it.

3. .... If you .... someone .... something, you tell them the details of it.

4. .... If you .... what you're doing, you continue doing it.

5. .... If you .... doing something, you are pleased that you are going to be doing it.

6. .... If you .... someone on the telephone, you succeed in contacting them.

7. .... If you .... criticism, people criticise you.

8. .... If you .... a time or event, you remember it.

9. .... If you .... someone, you do their job for them because they are not present.

10. .... Firms which .... production, produce less.

11. .... If you .... a conversation, you interrupt it.

12. .... If you finally .... doing something, you do it after a long delay.

13. .... If you .... something dangerous, you handle it in a careless, irresponsible way.

14. .... When you start a job and .... somebody, that person did the job before you.

15. .... If you .... some information, you give that information to someone, for example, the police.

16. .... If you .... an illness, you catch it.

Test yourself by covering the right-hand column.

Organising Verbs with Two Particles – 2

Complete each definition with one of the verbs below.

come up against	cut down on	get behind with	live up to
bring in on	fix up with	go along with	look down on
catch up on	get away with	go in for	look up to
come out in	get back at	grow out of	run out of

1. .... If you .... someone, you respect them.

2. .... When you .... a competition, you enter it.

3. .... If you .... patience, you have no patience left.

4. .... People who .... you consider you inferior.

5. .... If you .... a decision, you accept it.

6. .... When you .... a habit, you reach an age when you no longer have the habit.

7. .... When burglars .... something they have stolen, they escape with it.

8. .... If you .... some work, you do some work which you should have completed before.

9. .... If you .... someone .... a job, you arrange for them to have it.

10. .... If you .... your reputation, you show that you are as good as people expect you to be.

11. .... If you .... spots, they appear on your body.

12. .... If you .... the number of cigarettes you smoke, you don't smoke so many.

13. .... If you .... problems, you meet them and have to deal with them.

14. .... If you .... payments, you have not made them yet.

15. .... If you .... someone .... a discussion, you involve them in it.

16. .... If someone has done something wrong to you and you .... them, you get revenge in some way.

Test yourself by covering the right-hand column. Pay special attention to the word order with these verbs with two particles.

BE

1 The verb BE is used in combination with some of the particles studied in this book. Often the particles have similar meanings to those they have when combined with other verbs. Complete each sentence with one of the following particles. Use each item once only.

down   down with   in   off   on   out   out of   up

1. Well, I'm .... now. See you tomorrow morning.

2. No wonder they're celebrating! Profits are .... by 90%!

3. Have you got any red peppers?
   – I'm afraid we're .... them at the moment but we'll have some more in tomorrow.

4. My father's been very .... since he lost his job.

5. I hear the boss is ill.
   – That's right he's .... flu.

6. Have you given her your entry form yet? They must be .... by the end of the week.

7. Let's have a look around the shops. There are a lot of sales .... at the moment.

8. Can I speak to Mary, please?
   – I'm afraid she's .... at the moment but she should be back soon.

2 Now do the same with these sentences:

out   away   down   in   in on   off   on   up to   up

1. If Philip rings, tell him I'm ...., I won't be .... till next year!

2. Things are really bad. Sales are .... by 50%
   so far this year and it doesn't look as if the situation is
   going to improve.

3. When does she come back from her business trip?
   – She's .... until Friday.

4. Oh dear! This yoghurt tastes strange.
   I think it's ....

5. Nigel's still in bed.
   – Why isn't he .... yet? His alarm went
   ages ago.

6. No wonder the car won't start! The handbrake
   is still .... !

7. I joined the team at a later stage. I wasn't
   .... any of the original discussions.

8. What on earth do you think you're ....?
   – Nothing – really – nothing!

"Why aren't you up yet!"

COME

1 **Complete each sentence using the correct form of the verb COME and the particles given. Use each particle once only.**

across   down   in   out   over   round   up   up with   on

1. We had to call off the picnic because the rain was .... so heavily.

2. I think I'll keep that piece of wood. It might .... useful one day.

3. Soaking the pullover in this solution should make the stain ....

4. Fiona fainted, and when she ...., she found herself in hospital.

5. While I was tidying out the cupboard, I .... these old magazines.

6. Darren suddenly started yelling and screaming. I don't know what .... him.

7. We left early the next morning, just as the sun was ....

8. Oh ....! Hurry up! It's time you .... the answer.

"The sun is coming up!"

2 **Now do the same with these sentences:**

across   in for   into   off   on   out in   up from

1. Of course, appearances can be deceptive, but she .... as a very confident person, doesn't she?

2. I'd better take one of my pills. I think I've got a migraine .... and I want to stop it getting too bad.

3. When her parents died, Edith .... a lot of money.

4. You can tell by his accent that he .... Wales.

5. I think I'm allergic to certain kinds of seafood because I suddenly .... spots after I'd eaten some.

6. People didn't like the way the Minister handled the situation and he .... a lot of criticism.

7. The room was in a terrible state. The wallpaper was .... the walls so we had to stick it on again.

8. Did the subject .... in the course of conversation?
   – No. It wasn't mentioned at all.

GET

1 Match the two halves of each dialogue. Write your answers in the boxes.

1. Everyone seems to know about your engagement.	A Don't let her comments get to you. It's not that bad.
2. Have you found a job yet!	B Very nice. We get on with them really well.
3. Why do you want a pay-rise?	C I'm afraid not – and it's really getting me down.
4. What are your new neighbours like?	D As it's his first offence, he may get off with a fine.
5. Do you think Nick will go to prison?	E There's no rush. The train doesn't get in for another twenty minutes.
6. It's time you had a holiday.	F I know. The news has certainly got around.
7. Hayley didn't think much of my painting, did she?	G Because I can't get by on my salary any more.
8. Shouldn't we be leaving for the station?	H I know, but we can't get away till November.

1		2		3		4		5		6		7		8	

2 Now do the same with these dialogues:

1. How did the prisoners manage to escape?	A In that case you'd better get in an electrician.
2. George is still in bed.	B They got out through a window.
3. Do you think Barbara will be able to persuade him to pay?	C Can't you get out of it and come swimming instead?
4. I don't understand how this lighting system works.	D I've been too busy – I simply haven't got round to it.
5. Shall I give you your injection now, Mr Petrie?	E All right, nurse. Let's get it over with.
6. This is the right bus for the station, isn't it?	F She should do. She knows how to get round him.
7. Have you fixed your car yet?	G That's right. Get off at the next stop.
8. I've got to help in the shop this afternoon.	H What! Hasn't he got up yet?

1		2		3		4		5		6		7		8	

Now underline all the phrasal verbs.

GO

1 **Complete the sentences by using the correct form of the verb GO and the particles below. Use each particle once only.**

about   ahead   by   down   down with   off   through   up

1. If you don't keep yoghurt in the fridge in the summer, it will soon ....

2. At the beginning of the play, the curtain .... and the audience saw a woman standing alone in the centre of the stage.

3. We became more and more concerned as time .... and we didn't hear any news.

4. I'm not surprised she looked so frightened. It was a terrifying experience to ....

5. We've got the green light. We can .... and make the changes we wanted.

6. Geoffrey won't be coming to the meeting this evening. He has .... a virus.

7. How was the news received?
   – I'm afraid it didn't .... very well.

8. You'll never solve problems by shouting at people. You're .... this in completely the wrong way.

2 **Now do the same with these sentences:**

for   into   off   on   out   up   with   without

1. The burglars panicked and ran away when the alarm ....

2. Please don't stop. .... with your story.

3. It's a difficult choice but I think I'll .... the second option.

4. What do you think of this handbag?
   – The colour isn't right. It doesn't .... your dress.

5. Let's talk about your proposal for giving students more homework.
   – I don't want to .... that at the moment. I'll discuss it later.

6. If prices .... any more, I won't be able to pay my rent.

"Going without sleep . . . burning the candle at both ends!"

7. What are you doing this evening?
   – I'm .... to the cinema with my boyfriend.

8. You need more sleep. If you keep .... it, your health will suffer.

PUT

1 Match the two halves of each dialogue. Write your answers in the boxes.

1. That's a dreadful noise, isn't it?

2. Philip isn't clever enough to plan such a crime on his own.

3. Where are you staying?

4. Can't you concentrate on your work?

5. I don't want to be a nuisance.

6. What terrible news! How did he take it?

7. What's your next performance going to be?

8. I don't like the look of this place!

A He put on a brave face but he was obviously upset.

B We're putting on `Romeo and Juliet' in October.

C No. The noise is putting me off.

D Don't be put off by the outside. It's really nice inside.

E Yes, I'm not putting up with it any longer, I'm going to complain.

F A friend has offered to put me up for the night.

G Don't worry! You're not putting me out at all.

H You're right. Someone must have put him up to it.

1		2		3		4		5		6		7		8	

2 Now do the same with these dialogues:

1. Could I speak to Mary White, please?

2. Our poor dog is in terrible pain.

3. Hurry up or we'll be late!

4. Can I borrow the scissors?

5. I'm starting to get a bit cold now.

6. Rita's got some new proposals for ways of saving money.

7. What kind of an increase have you asked for?

8. Why did Leo have to buy a new suit?

A She should put them forward at the next meeting.

B One moment, please. I'll put you through to her office.

C Well, put your pullover on.

D Because he's put on so much weight recently.

E We've put in for a pay rise of ten per cent.

F You'd better have him put down and end his suffering.

G Nearly ready. I've just got to put these plates away.

H OK, but make sure you put them back when you've finished with them.

1		2		3		4		5		6		7		8	

Now go through the sentences on the right and underline the phrasal verbs.

TAKE

1 **Complete the sentences by using the correct form of the verb TAKE and the particles below. Use each particle once only.**

away   back   down   off   on   out   to   up

1. Trevor has threatened to take you to court if you don't .... what you said.

2. After being in several amateur productions, I decided to .... acting professionally.

3. When we arrived at the airport, the plane had already ....

4. Sales of our products increased dramatically so we had to .... extra staff to keep up with the demand.

5. We want to buy a new car, but it will mean .... a loan, and we want to avoid that.

6. The concert was last week but they still haven't .... the posters from the notice boards.

7. The sea and the sky looked so beautiful that they .... my breath ....

8. Irma was pleasant enough but I never really .... her. Maybe it was because we seemed to have nothing in common.

2 **Now do the same with these sentences:**

aback   after   apart   back   in   off   on   over

1. With that nose of hers, Nathalie certainly .... her father – and she's got his temper too!

2. One of the first things I learnt in the army was how to .... a gun .... and then put it together again.

3. Seeing those tall chimneys over there .... me .... to my childhood when I lived in a town with a lot of heavy industry.

4. Many employees lost their jobs when the firm was .... by a large multi-national company.

5. Helena was wearing such strange clothes that we were all .... It took us some time to get over the shock.

"Taken aback by her appearance!"

6. You look exhausted. I think you've .... more than you can handle.

7. If you're so cold, ... that thin shirt and put on something warmer.

8. He fooled most people into believing that he was a policeman. I suppose they were .... by the uniform.

BRING and TURN

1 **Match the two halves of each dialogue. Write your answers in the boxes.**

BRING

1. I've got some photos I took of the excursion to London.

A Why not? We've tried to bring them up to be independent.

2. What caused the rash?

B Only if you promise to bring it back before the weekend!

3. What new books have you got planned for next year?

C It must have been brought on by some kind of allergy.

4. Can I borrow your ladder for a while?

D It certainly was. It brought back memories of my stay in Rome.

5. Would you let your children go camping on their own?

E Apparently, it took them ages to bring her round.

6. Was Miriam unconscious for very long?

F We're going to bring out a series on famous painters.

7. Will the Opposition parties work together?

G Great! You must bring them along to the next meeting.

8. That was an interesting film about Italy, wasn't it?

H They'll have to if they want to bring down the Government.

1		2		3		4		5		6		7		8	

2 **Now do the same with these dialogues:**

TURN

1. What happened to the theatre in the centre of town?

A The road was blocked so I had to turn back and find another route.

2. Whatever made you ask someone like him for help?

B So did I but it turned out sunny in the end.

3. Did Jill accept your suggestion?

C It was turned into a cinema.

4. Don't you think it's a bit cold in here?

D Yes they did. They turned up an hour late!

5. So, did the Maxwells come to the party after all?

E Yes, it is a bit chilly. Turn the heating on if you want to.

6. Why did it take you so long to drive here?

F There was nobody else I could turn to.

7. Are you watching that film?

G No. She turned it down.

8. I thought it was going to rain.

H No, I'm not. Shall I turn it off?

1		2		3		4		5		6		7		8	

KEEP and LOOK

1 **Match the two halves of each dialogue. Write your answers in the boxes.**

KEEP

1. I'm afraid of getting bitten by mosquitoes.

2. Has he told you everything he knows about the robbery?

3. How did you manage to sell more than your competitors?

4. This course is really difficult.

5. And don't forget that you promised to mend that chair.

6. What happened to that car you were buying?

7. Why does Annabel buy so many women's magazines?

8. How careful do you have to be about what you eat?

A They took it back. I couldn't keep up the payments.

B I keep off spicy foods, but apart from that I can eat anything.

C OK. I'll do it. Just don't keep on about it all the time.

D I don't think so. I'm sure he's keeping something back.

E She says she wants to keep up with the latest fashions.

F Keep at it! I'm sure it'll be worth all the effort in the end.

G Take this cream. It's supposed to keep them away.

H By keeping our prices down when they put theirs up.

1		2		3		4		5		6		7		8	

2 **Now do the same with these dialogues:**

LOOK

1. I don't know what this word means.

2. Have you found somewhere to live yet?

3. What's happening to your dogs while you're away on holiday?

4. They're so snobbish, aren't they?

5. Any news about your stolen video recorder?

6. Didn't Mandy say "Hello" when she saw you?

7. I wonder if Sandra's feeling any better.

8. Only two more weeks and then we're on holiday.

A I know. I'm really looking forward to having a break.

B No. She looked straight through me and pretended I wasn't there.

C Yes. They look down on people like you and me.

D Well, look it up in a dictionary.

E We've looked round a few flats but they're all too expensive.

F The police are looking into it but they aren't very hopeful.

G My mother-in-law's looking after them.

H I'll look in on the way home and see how she is.

1		2		3		4		5		6		7		8	

83

Unit 73

Organising Common Verbs – 1

Complete each of the groups of sentences by using one of the following verbs. Use each verb once only.

get   go   is   keep   look

1.

I have to		off fatty foods.
I wish he wouldn't		on about his new car all the time.
He likes to		up with the latest news.
These lights should		away any burglars.
Why should he		back such vital information?
They weren't able to		up the payments on their car.

2.

I'm afraid he		out at the moment but he'll be back soon.
I'm sure this milk		off. Here, you smell it.
The television		on but I can't hear any sound.
OK. Time		up. Can I have your answer, please?
The price of chicken		down this week.
My application		in so I hope to get an interview.

3.

It's nice to		forward to your holidays, isn't it!
Remember to		up any words you don't know.
Could you		after our cat while we're away?
Why don't you		in on her on your way to work?
They're snobs. They		down on pupils from my school.
The police must		into lots of similar crimes every year.

4.

Why did that alarm		off?
I never want to		through such an experience again.
Don't stop. Please		on with your work.
Would you like to		out for a meal this evening?
We'll have to		through with it. We can't pull out!
Which option will he		for?

5.

I'll have to		up early tomorrow morning.
When does her train		in?
It's important to		on well with your colleagues.
Try not to let the criticism		to you.
If I can't do it myself, I'll		an electrician in.
She can just		by on her salary and no more.

Use this page to test yourself.

84

Organising Common Verbs – 2

Complete each of the groups of sentences by using one of the following verbs. Use each verb once only.

bring   come   put   take   turn

1.
He had to		up two children on his own.
When are you going to		back those tools I lent you?
Eating tomatoes may		on that rash again.
Writing books doesn't		in much money.
She wants to		along a friend when we go out.
These photos		back memories of my holiday.

2.
The dentist had to		out two teeth.
With that red hair they		after their mother.
We usually		on extra staff in the summer.
Please		off your jacket if you want to.
Will you help me		down those notices?
You should		up some kind of sport to keep fit.

3.
Unfortunately, I		on weight during my holiday.
The employees have		in for a pay rise.
Don't be		off by his clothes. He's really very nice.
She		forward her proposal at the meeting.
I try to		by a little money each week.
I just can't		up with these arguments any longer!

4.
The weather didn't		out too bad after all.
We'll have to		back. The road's blocked.
Can I		on the TV and watch the film?
He didn't		up although he'd promised to come.
Who else could I		to for help?
They usually		down any applicants who are over forty.

5.
That box might		in useful one day.
He expects to		into a lot of money very soon.
The subject didn't		up in the course of our discussion.
They		across as really nice people, don't they.
Have you		up with a solution to our problem?
Will the stain		out if I wash it?

Now underline all the particles.

Business – 1

1 Complete each sentence with the correct form of one of the verbs below. Use each verb once only.

bring out	**close down**	**go ahead**	**take over**
build up	**cut back**	**put forward**	**think over**

1. Business was so bad that they had to .... two factories.

2. I .... my proposal at the meeting but it was rejected.

3. Next year we intend to .... several new products but at the moment we're still testing them.

4. Decisions would no longer be made locally if a big multi-national .... our company.

5. It was finally decided that the scheme should .... but with a few changes.

6. It took hard work to .... this company from nothing to what it is today.

7. Until we get some new orders we'll have to .... production.

8. Before I come to a decision I'll have to .... their offer very carefully.

2 Now do the same with these verbs:

branch out	**plan ahead**	**sell out**	**take off**
dry up	**run through**	**set up**	**take up**

1. We can't depend on just one type of product to be successful. We need to .... into other areas.

2. After his company went bankrupt, Frank .... another one in his wife's name.

3. There are still one or two things I'm not quite sure about. Could we just .... the details of our agreement once more?

4. Because of the advance publicity all copies of the new game had .... within an hour so the store had to order some more.

5. You really don't seem able to deal with my problem so I'll have to .... this matter .... with your head office.

6. Because of the transport strike, supplies .... and we had to stop production.

7. After it was recommended on television, sales of the shampoo really ....

8. We're already thinking about what we'll be selling in five years' time. In this business it's essential to ....

Business – 2

1 **Match an item on the left with an item on the right. Use each item once only. Write your answers in the boxes provided.**

1. bring forward   A   the company because we can't pay our debts.

2. carry out   B   the components we need to repair the car.

3. draw up   C   our supplier to chase the order.

4. ring up   D   production to meet increased demand.

5. run out of   E   the meeting from Friday to Wednesday.

6. step up   F   the contract and send you a copy.

7. wind up   G   the pros and cons before deciding.

8. weigh up   H   a survey into people's leisure activities.

1		2		3		4		5		6		7		8	

2 **Now do the same with these items:**

1. The chairman   A   dragged on and we seemed to be getting nowhere.

2. The company   B   came up to sell our goods abroad.

3. Competition   C   lay ahead but they managed to survive.

4. The deal   D   hotted up and we were forced to cut prices.

5. Difficult times   E   picked up after some initial difficulties.

6. The meeting   F   stepped down after doing the job for ten years.

7. An opportunity   G   went through and our jobs were saved.

8. Trade   H   went under and they all lost their jobs.

"I'm afraid they went under during the recession."

1		2		3		4		5		6		7		8	

Test yourself by covering one of the columns and trying to remember the other part.

Work

Choose the correct alternative to complete each sentence.

1. As business was bad, they had to .... some of their staff.
   A put down **B** lay off **C** take on **D** hang up

2. At last the recession seems to have ....
   A topped off **B** slimmed down **C** bogged down **D** bottomed out

3. Mary applied for the post but she was ....
   A turned down **B** checked out **C** kept under **D** pushed ahead

4. The workers decided to .... until their demands were met.
   A stand up **B** lie behind **C** sit in **D** sleep out

5. How are you .... in your new post?
   A getting on **B** going along
   C getting down **D** coming by

6. The union threatened to ....
   the workers on strike.
   A call out **B** ask up
   C hear out **D** see down

7. I'm so tired! I've been ....
   with work this week!
   A clogged up **B** snarled up
   C held down **D** snowed under

"I'm always snowed under in the middle of summer!"

8. On an impulse he .... his job and went abroad.
   A gave in **B** put off **C** threw up **D** set down

9. The staff .... in support of their pay claim.
   A fell off **B** walked out **C** kept back **D** turned off

10. If orders keep coming in like this, I'll have to .... more staff.
    A give up **B** add in **C** gain on **D** take on

11. His assistant had to .... for him the last time he was ill.
    A stand down **B** keep on **C** take on **D** fill in

12. Once again poor Colin has been .... for promotion.
    A stood by **B** passed over **C** locked out **D** struck off

13. If my working conditions don't improve, I'll .... my notice.
    A give up **B** fire off **C** hand in **D** give out

14. We're looking for someone who can .... with the rest of our team.
    A get up **B** fit in **C** act up **D** work off

Technology and Computing

1   Complete each sentence with the correct form of one of the verbs given. Use each verb once only.

cut out	**go through**	**stand up to**	**top up**
filter out	**read off**	**strip down**	**wire up**

1. This water pump has a special device on it to .... any impurities.

2. Something was wrong with the engine so we .... it .... and examined each part.

3. No wonder the fridge didn't work. You hadn't .... the plug correctly.

4. These machines need to be solid. They have to .... a lot of rough treatment.

5. The only maintenance that is required is to .... the oil if it gets a bit low.

6. Every time we start up the drilling machine we have to .... a strict safety procedure to prevent any accidents.

7. The operator monitors the pressure by .... the measurements on these gauges.

8. The engine kept .... and then starting again a few seconds later.

2   Now do the same with these verbs. The sentences are to do with computing.

back up	**put down to**	**set up**	**take up**
print out	**run out of**	**sift through**	**work out**

1. Check your work on the screen. Once you're satisfied, you can .... a copy.

2. If the printer .... paper, a warning light indicates that you need some more.

3. First you .... your database and then you type in your clients' records.

4. You give the computer a command and it will .... the data for you until it finds the information you need.

5. The boss said it was nobody's fault but we .... it .... bad programming on the part of those 'experts' at head office.

6. The program .... a lot of disk space so there wasn't much room for anything else.

7. Calculations which used to take ages can now be .... in a few seconds.

8. In case anything goes wrong with the computer, you should always .... any work you do and keep those disks in a safe place.

Travel and Transport

Choose the correct alternative to complete each sentence.

1. The plane should have .... at eleven o'clock but it was delayed.
   A set up **B** taken off **C** let on **D** opened out

2. The details of cancellation charges are .... in the table below.
   A held in **B** added up **C** set out **D** written up

3. We finally .... on our journey at two o'clock in the afternoon.
   A set off **B** went out **C** came up **D** got about

4. I have to .... at the airport two hours before departure.
   A check up **B** set down **C** sign on **D** check in

5. We got to the stop just as the coach was ....
   A taking off **B** making out **C** settling down **D** pulling away

6. Why don't you .... in Oxford on the way home?
   A stop off **B** take in **C** pass through **D** draw up

7. I went ashore at most of the ports we .... on our cruise.
   A pulled up **B** came about **C** put into **D** drew up

8. The road had .... and driving conditions were terrible.
   A slipped up **B** iced over
   C gummed up **D** splashed down

9. As the aircraft .... one of
   the wheels came off.
   A tripped up **B** put off
   C ran down **D** touched down

10. While Adam was cycling home, he was
    .... by a lorry.
    A driven out **B** speeded up
    C flown into **D** run down

11. We decided to .... in Athens
    for a few days on our way home.
    A stop over **B** put up **C** set up **D** close down

"Thank goodness I was able to slam on the brakes in time!"

12. Suddenly a taxi .... and an important-looking official got out.
    A drew up **B** called by **C** levelled out **D** stopped out

13. Our car .... just as we were crossing the bridge.
    A came out **B** broke down **C** cut back **D** shut down

14. A boy ran out into the road, but the driver .... his brakes just in time.
    A brought down **B** put in **C** sent out **D** slammed on

Health and Fitness

1   **Match an item on the left with an item on the right. Use each item once only. Write your answers in the boxes.**

1. come out in   A   your arm so you won't be able to use it.

2. get over   B   your muscles with these simple exercises.

3. put on   C   the operation and start work again.

4. strap up   D   a prescription for the patient.

5. take out   E   a sport to keep fit.

6. take up   F   a rash all over my chest.

7. tone up   G   weight if you eat such sweet food.

8. write out   H   my wisdom teeth if they hurt too much.

1		2		3		4		5		6		7		8	

2   **Now do the same with these items:**

1. The anaesthetic   A   cleared up when I took the antibiotics.

2. My ankle   B   fell out because he was so worried.

3. His hair   C   healed up but there's still a
                           small scar.

4. The infection   D   pulled through because she'd been
                           looked after so well.

5. The patient   E   settled down but I decided not to
                           eat for a while.

6. My stomach   F   shot up as the fever got worse.

7. Her temperature   G   swelled up and I couldn't put
                           my shoe on.

8. The wound   H   wore off but he felt very strange when he woke up.

"My hair is falling out with worry."

1		2		3		4		5		6		7		8	

Test yourself by covering one of the columns.

Sport and Leisure – 1

Choose the correct alternative to complete each sentence.

1. The team spent some time .... in preparation for the match.
   A running away   **B** warming up   **C** doing in   **D** winning through

2. The champion had a crowd of supporters to ....
   A bring her round   **B** cheer her on   **C** do her down   **D** give her up

3. The pond .... and the villagers were able to skate on it.
   A caved in   **B** stretched out   **C** snowed off   **D** froze over

4. I want to get the garden tidy before winter ....
   A sets out   **B** sets in   **C** hangs about   **D** falls off

5. Some supporters were .... at the entrance because the ground was full.
   A sent off   **B** turned away   **C** set out   **D** played off

6. The show is so popular that it's .... for weeks ahead.
   A put out   **B** checked in   **C** booked up   **D** shut down

7. The committee want us to .... the entertainment for the social evening.
   A lay on   **B** sit on   **C** put down   **D** settle down

8. It was such a bad foul that the referee
   ....
   A cut him up   **B** sent him off
   C did him up   **D** used him up

9. If the rain .... we might
   still be able to play the match.
   A eases up   **B** sets off
   C hots up   **D** fires away

10. The band .... and the
    dancers made their way to the floor.
    A played off   **B** struck out
    C struck up   **D** beat out

    "Off!"

11. When the applause had .... the star of the show said a few words.
    A stepped forward   **B** gone out   **C** played through   **D** died down

12. I had to keep .... new things for the children to do during their
    holiday. They got bored so easily!
    A dreaming up   **B** running down   **C** acting up   **D** passing through

13. Maggie's been .... her game and you can see a definite improvement.
    A sitting for   **B** working on   **C** checking in   **D** trying on

14. The match was .... and will be played next Wednesday.
    A pelted down   **B** poured out   **C** rained off   **D** seen through

Sport and Leisure – 2

1 Match an item on the left with an item on the right. Use each item once only. Write your answers in the boxes.

1.	Many cinemas	A	blared out and we couldn't hear ourselves speak.
2.	The curtain	B	caught on and soon everyone was doing it.
3.	The dance	C	closed down when television became popular.
4.	The golfers	D	fell off when another club opened.
5.	Membership	E	teed off but both played terrible shots.
6.	The music	F	tuned up and waited for the conductor to arrive.
7.	The musicians	G	played off to decide third place.
8.	The two teams	H	came down and the booing began!

1		2		3		4		5		6		7		8	

2 Now do the same with these items:

1.	carry off	A	the committee and help to make decisions.
2.	plant out	B	this dance because my feet are killing me.
3.	play through	C	a hobby to help you relax after work.
4.	put on	D	this tune once and then you try to sing it.
5.	sit on	E	the prize for the most beautiful garden.
6.	sit out	F	the seedlings when they're big enough.
7.	soak up	G	a show twice a year.
8.	take up	H	the sun as you lie on the beach.

"Soaking up the sun."

1		2		3		4		5		6		7		8	

Test yourself by covering over one of the columns.

Feelings and Emotions – 1

Choose the correct alternative to complete each sentence.

1. They were .... with excitement at the thought of seeing the sea.
   A acting out **B** bubbling over **C** jumping on **D** sweeping away

2. What made Wayne so angry? He .... with a face as black as thunder!
   A rained off **B** stormed out **C** snowed under **D** iced over

3. The crowd seemed very unenthusiastic so the MC tried to .... some excitement.
   A beat out **B** strike up **C** whip up **D** hit on

4. Miles had a lot of emotional problems but we managed to ....
   A lay him off **B** straighten him out **C** send him up **D** find him out

5. When the children saw the ice-cream stall, their eyes ....
   A cheered up **B** cried out **C** revolved around **D** lit up

6. We were so upset that we could hardly .... the tears.
   A hold back **B** keep off **C** set off **D** step down

7. You know they're only trying to make you lose your temper! .... !
   A Simmer down **B** Eat away **C** Work out **D** Tuck in

8. Derek was so angry at the news that he .... the phone and rushed out of the room.
   A called up **B** hung on **C** slammed down **D** rang off

9. Stewart will soon change his mind. I know how to .... him.
   A tell on **B** pick through **C** centre on **D** get round

10. Nicole's been in a mood for days now. I wished she'd .... it.
    A snap out of **B** mess about with **C** look down on **D** show through

11. We don't usually act like that. We got .... by the excitement of the occasion.
    A moved on **B** strung up **C** pointed out **D** carried away

12. The smell of hot buttered toast .... me back to my childhood.
    A holds **B** takes **C** gives **D** sets

13. Marcia's dog was killed by a car and it took her some time to .... the shock.
    A get over **B** do without **C** come round **D** fill out

14. When Nancy saw the mess the burglar had left, she .... in tears.
    A went under **B** came apart **C** wiped off **D** broke down

Feelings and Emotions – 2

Choose the correct alternative to complete each sentence.

1. When Helen and Andrew saw how ridiculous they looked they .... laughing.
   A came round **B** burst out **C** broke in **D** flowed over

2. When he saw her with John, Jack .... anger.
   A showed up **B** bristled with **C** pricked with **D** brushed with

3. Christine felt that she was among friends so she ....a little.
   A looked up **B** melted away **C** opened up **D** screwed up

4. Sonja and Shirley haven't spoken to each other since they .... two years ago.
   A fell out **B** stepped back **C** mixed up **D** died down

5. I hate Joan Clifford! One day I'll .... for all the pain she's caused!
   A sound her out **B** show her off **C** tell her apart **D** pay her back

6. Eva doesn't care what she says. People are often .... by her outspoken comments.
   A set aside **B** taken aback **C** stood over **D** taken off

7. Ben's so unlucky in love. Why does he .... the type of woman who brings trouble?
   A catch on **B** fall for **C** put before **D** set out

8. When Howard saw the broken window, he .... a rage.
   A flew into   **B** drove out
   C faced up to **D** steamed off

9. Terry's quite nice really. Don't be .... by his appearance.
   A checked off **B** put off
   C set on   **D** taken over

10. Molly just couldn't cope with his moods any more so they ....
    A split up   **B** got by
    C tore apart **D** fell through

"Mum, this is Terry. Don't let his appearance put you off. He's really nice."

11. Roy got very emotional. I don't know what .... him.
    A went under **B** sawed through **C** got out of **D** came over

12. Yvonne didn't know what to do. She was .... by conflicting emotions.
    A torn apart **B** split off **C** burnt down **D** chopped up

13. Bill and Ted .... each other straightaway and became firm friends.
    A took after **B** held together **C** took to **D** let in

14. I try to be friendly but I find it hard to .... some of my younger colleagues.
    A get up to **B** come up with **C** get on with **D** get by on

Law and Order – 1

Choose the best alternative to complete the sentence.

1. When Bruce .... the judge, he continued to protest that he was innocent.
   A argued out **B** came before **C** saw to **D** swore by

2. Some of the people on the march were trying to .... trouble.
   A egg on **B** fill up **C** stir up **D** toughen up

3. We had to pay a lot of money in damages after the verdict .... us.
   A came up against **B** delivered up **C** threw off **D** went against

4. When I returned, I found my car had been .... by the police.
   A fitted up **B** gathered up **C** taken after **D** towed away

5. From the witnesses' stories we managed to .... what had happened.
   A answer to **B** bring up **C** piece together **D** turn over

6. With a smart lawyer you might .... just a fine.
   A get away with **B** get down to **C** go in for **D** do away with

7. Lesley's being very secretive. I'm sure she's .... something dishonest.
   A carried forward **B** fallen out with **C** mixed up in **D** joined up

8. The police arrested several well-known criminals after .... a tip-off.
   A acting on **B** adhering to **C** marking off **D** showing up

9. For the third time this year the bank has been ....
   A balanced out **B** held up **C** shot down **D** stolen away

10. The prisoners .... their cells and climbed on the roof.
    A came in on **B** broke out of **C** got away with **D** went out on

11. The police will have to .... security for the President's visit.
    A loosen up **B** tie down **C** tighten up **D** weed out

12. Many people were wounded after the terrorists started .... with machine guns.
    A blazing away **B** falling off **C** shouting out **D** whipping out

13. We have .... our inquiries after receiving new information.
    A added up **B** enlarged on **C** pushed around **D** stepped up

14. Mark's been .... for questioning about a series of muggings.
    A joined in **B** joined up **C** spoken for **D** taken in

Law and Order – 2

Choose the best alternative to complete the sentence.

1. By the way the judge ...., you could see he thought they were guilty.
   A measured up **B** pointed out **C** summed up **D** weighed against

2. The police don't think they'll ever .... all the missing money.
   A find for **B** put down to **C** rip off **D** track down

3. The prisoner's been .... in a cell for 4 days so he may be more willing to talk.
   A cooped up **B** put through **C** sent up **D** tidied away

4. The house was .... and some valuable paintings were stolen.
   A broken into **B** slipped up **C** stolen away **D** worked at

5. Instead of .... the crooks, the guards just stood around in a daze.
   A blasting off **B** coming up with **C** going after **D** pulling on

6. If we .... this robbery, we'll be rich beyond our wildest dreams.
   A do away with **B** hold up **C** pull off **D** settle down

7. A man .... the robber's description was seen leaving the station.
   A answering to **B** looking on **C** seeing to **D** sticking with

8. You must tell the police what you know! .... information is a criminal offence.
   A Answering back **B** Holding back **C** Putting forward **D** Setting up

9. One of the gang .... the others. How else could the police have known?
   A covered up **B** ganged up on **C** informed on **D** spoke out

10. We were holding up the traffic so the policeman told us to ....
    A come forth **B** move on **C** run out **D** tail back

11. The judgement was .... and she was able to return to her family.
    A put away **B** set aside **C** taken aback **D** worn out

12. June won't be going to prison. The judge .... with just a caution this time.
    A let her off **B** picked her up **C** set her up **D** turned her down

13. The police are .... a spate of burglaries in the area.
    A looking out for **B** looking into **C** seeing off **D** taking down

14. We're sure these people are guilty but we can't .... them without proof.
    A act on **B** lean over **C** lock in on **D** proceed against

Colloquial Expressions – 1

1 **Match one half of the dialogue on the left with its response on the right. Use each half once only. Write your answers in the boxes.**

Only a genius can do this exercise! ▶ **Come off it! It's not that difficult!**

1. Well, the thing is ... I don't quite know how to put this.

A Are you sure she wasn't putting it on?

2. I hear you aren't going out with Bill any more.

B That must have set you back a bit!

3. We stayed at the best hotel in town.

C He really lays it on a bit thick, doesn't he?

4. Ryan says she's the most beautiful girl he's ever seen.

D Come on. Spit it out. I won't get annoyed.

5. How did he react when he failed his driving test?

E That's right. We just didn't hit it off.

6. Lorraine sounded very ill.

F He was really cut up about it.

1		2		3		4		5		6	

2 **Now do the same with these dialogues:**

1. Do you think Jenny really sent him those flowers?

A Get away! He doesn't look more than thirty.

2. How about a kiss, then?

B Sure! Fire away!

3. They always manage to make a a success of whatever they do.

C Yes, but it really takes it out of you. I was exhausted!

4. Can I ask you a question?

D I wouldn't put it past her.

5. Oliver says he's got three grandchildren.

E They certainly do. You've got to hand it to them, haven't you?

6. Did you enjoy your climb?

F Cut it out! You're old enough to be my father!

1		2		3		4		5		6	

Now underline all the phrasal verbs.

Colloquial Expressions – 2

1   **Match one half of the dialogue on the left with the other half on the right. Write your answers in the boxes.**

What happened when the brick hit him?   ▶   **He went out like a light.**

1. The scenery was magnificent, wasn't it?

A   He put on a brave face, but you could see he was upset.

2. Those children are making a terrible noise!

B   He'll come down on me like a ton of bricks.

3. What will happen when the boss finds out about the mix-up?

C   If she does, they'll soon cut her down to size.

4. What was the midnight movie like?

D   They're only letting off steam.

5. Do you think Martha will try to boss them around?

E   Really terrifying. It scared the pants off me!

6. How did he react when she walked out on him?

F   It certainly was. It took my breath away.

1		2		3		4		5		6	

2   **Now do the same with these dialogues:**

1. Was Clifford pleased when you pointed out his mistakes?

A   That's true, but we just seemed to run out of steam.

2. What happened when Gail got home so late?

B   With those expensive clothes, it stands out a mile.

3. So they've made up, have they?

C   Not exactly! He told me where to get off!

4. But you were all so enthusiastic when you started.

D   No, I didn't. I kept trying, but in the end I gave it up as a bad job.

5. Did you manage to get through to him eventually?

E   Well, of course, her parents went off the deep end.

6. How do know Blanche is rich?

F   Yes. Now they're getting on like a house on fire.

1		2		3		4		5		6	

Now underline all the phrasal verbs.

Phrasal Verb Nouns – 1

Complete each pair of sentences by using one verb and one noun from the list below.

break down	breakdown	hold up	hold-up
break out	outbreak	print out	print-out
burst out	outburst	stand in	stand-in
clean up	clean-up	take off	take-off
drop out	drop-out	warm up	warm-up

1. Press that key and the computer will .... the figures you need.

   Press that key and you'll get a .... of the figures you need.

2. We do stretching exercises to .... before starting the work-out.

   We do stretching exercises as a .... before starting the work-out.

3. They .... laughing when they saw Len was wearing odd socks.

   There was an .... of laughter when they saw Len was wearing odd socks.

4. While the robbers were .... the bank, someone sounded the alarm.

   During the ...., someone sounded the alarm.

5. Because of all the stress Silvia .... and had to go into hospital.

   Because of the stress Silvia had a nervous .... and went into hospital.

"We all burst out laughing at his socks!"

6. You aren't allowed to smoke while the plane is ....

   You aren't allowed to smoke during ....

7. Those who .... of university were looked down on by the others.

   Any university .... were looked down on by the other students.

8. The fighting .... soon after the assassination attempt.

   There was an .... of fighting soon after the assassination attempt.

9. The star has someone who .... for him in any dangerous scenes.

   The star of the film has a .... for any dangerous scenes.

10. This room is in a mess. You should .... it .... and get rid of all the rubbish.

    This room is in a mess. It needs a good ....

It will help you to understand and remember these nouns more easily if you learn them together with the original phrasal verb, where possible.

Phrasal Verb Nouns – 2

Complete each pair of sentences by using a verb and a noun from the list below.

bring up	upbringing	stand by	stand-by
build up	build-up	stop over	stopover
check in	check-in	stow away	stowaway
pass by	passer-by	take over	takeover
shut down	shut-down	walk out	walk-out

1. They had to .... the power station to prevent any leak of radioactivity.

   He ordered an immediate .... to prevent any leak of radioactivity.

2. Her parents .... Ethel .... to know the difference between right and wrong.

   As a result of her ...., Ethel has strong sense of the difference between right and wrong.

3. The gas .... and we were afraid there would be an explosion.

   There was a .... of gas and we were afraid there would be an explosion.

4. As the flight is so long, why not .... in Singapore for a while?

   As the flight is so long, why not make a .... in Singapore?

5. After the firm was ...., several employees lost their jobs.

   After the ...., several employees lost their jobs.

6. A nurse was .... the scene of the accident, and she gave first aid.

   One of the .... was a nurse, and she gave first aid.

7. One person had boarded the ship in Cairo and .... amongst the cargo.

   A .... had boarded the ship in Cairo and hidden amongst the cargo.

8. We need you to .... so you can fill in if someone doesn't turn up.

   We need you on .... so you can fill in if someone doesn't turn up.

9. The employees .... in protest against the poor working conditions.

   There was a .... in protest against the poor working conditions.

10. You have to .... at the airport two hours before the plane leaves.

    .... is two hours before the plane leaves.

*Don't forget that the plural of **passer-by** is **passers-by**!*

101

Phrasal Verb Nouns – 3

Complete each pair of sentences by using one verb and one noun from the list below.

get away	getaway	look on	onlooker
get together	get-together	slip up	slip-up
go ahead	go-ahead	slow down	slowdown
hand over	hand-over	tail back	tailback
lay out	layout	tell off	telling-off

1. The crooks .... from the police in a helicopter.

   The crooks made their .... in a helicopter.

2. We're worried about violence when the army generals .... power to the new government.

   We're worried about violence during the .... of power to the new government.

3. The garden has been .... in this way to provide access for the disabled.

   The .... has been designed to provide access for the disabled.

4. Unfortunately, output has .... recently because of illness.

   Unfortunately, there has been a .... in output recently.

5. The person making the arrangements had .... so I missed my flight.

   There was a .... in the arrangements so I missed my flight.

6. The people who were .... cheered as they saw Anne being rescued from the sea.

   The .... cheered as they saw Anne being rescued from the sea.

7. The boss said we could .... and order the new photocopier.

   We got the .... from the boss to order the new photocopier.

8. Last night we .... at my house to plan the party.

   Last night we had a .... at my house to plan the party.

9. His aunt .... Hugh .... for making so much noise.

   She gave Hugh a .... for making so much noise.

10. Last weekend the traffic .... for 3 miles on the motorway.

    There was a 3-mile .... of traffic on the motorway.

"I've never seen a tailback like it!"

In the second sentence of each pair, notice the verb which makes the partnership with the phrasal verb noun: **get** *the go-ahead,* **have** *a get-together.*

Phrasal Verb Nouns – 4

Complete each pair of sentences by using one verb and one noun from the list below.

black out	blackout	lay out	outlay
change over	change-over	tip off	tip-off
kick off	kick-off	turn out	turn-out
knock out	knock-out	wash up	washing-up
rise up	uprising	work out	work-out

1. The champion .... his opponent in the second round.

   It's a .... and the champ wins in the second round!

2. Last night's power cut .... most of the city.

   Last night's power cut caused a .... in most of the city.

3. There were a few problems when we .... from the old to the new system of issuing library books.

   There were a few problems during the .... to the new system.

4. Someone had .... the police .... about the robbery and they were waiting for the thieves.

   The police had received a .... about the robbery.

5. If you .... , I'll dry.

   If you do the ...., I'll dry.

6. The President was forced to leave the country when the people .... against the government.

   There was an .... by the people against the government.

7. Soon after our team had .... they scored the first goal.

   Soon after the .... our team scored the first goal.

8. We have................................ over £100,000 on television advertising.

   The .... on television advertising has been over £100,000.

9. I keep fit by .... in the gym every day.

   To keep fit I have a .... in the gym every day.

10. Not many people .... to see the procession.

    There wasn't much of a .... to see the procession.

"Our daily work-out."

Phrasal Verb Adjectives – 1

Complete each pair of sentences by using one verb and one adjective from the list below.

build up	**built-up**	**run away**	**runaway**
cut off	**cut-off**	**stand out**	**outstanding**
knock down	**knockdown**	**tense up**	**tensed-up**
make up	**made-up**	**throw away**	**throwaway**
roll up	**rolled-up**	**wear out**	**worn out**

1. The fly was annoying him so he .... a newspaper and tried to hit it.

   The fly was annoying him so he tried to hit it with a .... newspaper.

2. Gwen was wearing a pair of jeans which she had .... just above the knee.

   Gwen was wearing a pair of .... jeans.

3. We couldn't control the bull, which .... and headed for the main road.

   There was panic as the .... bull headed for the main road.

4. We ought to recycle things we use, not .... them ....

   We live in a .... society. There are so many things we could re-use.

5. Dee's one of the best. She .... as one of the great actresses of this century.

   Dee's fantastic – one of the .... actresses of this century.

6. Relax. Try not to .... so much.

   You're all .... Try to relax.

7. I wasn't taken in. He'd obviously .... that story.

   I wasn't taken in by what was obviously a .... story.

8. Why does jogging leave you full of energy but .... me .... ?

   Why are you full of energy after jogging while I'm so .... ?

9. There's nowhere for children to play now this area's been so ....

   There's nowhere for children to play in a .... area like this.

10. After some bargaining I managed to .... the price of the chair by ten pounds.

    I did some bargaining and bought this chair at a .... price.

"Absolutely worn-out!"

As with the nouns, it is a good idea to learn these adjectives together with their original verb.

The adjectives on this page are more common than the verbs. Notice in No. 2 **cut-off** *jeans can also be called* **cut-down** *jeans.*

Phrasal Verb Adjectives – 2

Complete each pair of sentences by using one verb and one adjective from the list below.

break away	breakaway	sit down	sit-down
come in	incoming	speak out	outspoken
knock out	knockout	start up	start-up
pick up	pick-up	tire out	tired out
put off	off-putting	touch up	touched-up

1. Most of the flights were .... late so we didn't know when she would arrive.

   Most of the .... flights were late because of a strike.

2. One group disagreed with the leader, ... and formed their own party.

   One group, who disagreed with the leader, formed a .... party.

3. The protestors .... in the middle of the road and refused to move.

   They staged a .... protest in the middle of the road.

4. Percy hopes someone will lend him the capital to .... his business.

   Percy hopes someone will lend him the .... capital for his business.

5. They have .... the photo of the President to make him look much younger.

   The President is much older then this! This is clearly a .... photo!

6. I didn't get very far in the competition. I was .... in the first round.

   It was a .... competition and unfortunately I didn't get past the first round.

7. I fell down so many times on my skiing holiday that it .... me .... ever going on one again.

   After such an .... experience, I'll never go on a skiing holiday again!

"An off-putting experience!"

8. The coach kept stopping on the way to the port to .... passengers.

   There were several .... points on the way to the port.

9. It looks as if doing all that hard work has really .... John ....

   John looks really .... after doing all that hard work.

10. Barbara wasn't afraid to .... and criticise government policy.

   Barbara was an .... critic of government policy.

The adjectives on this page are more common than the verbs.

Opposites – 1

Complete each pair of sentences by using two phrasal verbs that are opposite in meaning. Choose from the pairs of verbs listed below.

knock out	bring round	slow down	speed up
look down on	look up to	stand up	sit down
pass out	come to	stay in	go out
put back	bring forward	switch on	switch off
set out	get back	turn up	turn down

1. I can't hear what she's saying. Can you .... the volume?

   I'm not deaf! Please .... the volume .... a bit!

2. The room was so stuffy that Paul ....

   Paul was unconscious for at least ten minutes before he ....

3. I can't go dancing every night! I'm going to .... tonight and watch TV.

   Watching TV is boring! Let's .... for a change and see a film, or something.

4. It's a very early start. We .... on our excursion at seven o'clock.

   Don't wait up for me. I won't .... from the excursion until midnight.

5. Sharon wanted to listen to the news so she .... the radio.

   The programme wasn't very good so Tracy .... the radio.

6. The punch was so powerful that it .... Frank .... for five minutes.

   They tried everything they knew to .... the boxer ....

7. We saw the car .... and almost come to a stop.

   The car began to .... and was soon going too fast to follow.

8. They were such snobs! They .... anyone they thought had come from an inferior school.

   I thought Kirk was marvellous. I .... him as my hero and tried to be like him.

9. The meeting's going to be later than originally planned. They've .... it .... from the 15th to the 18th.

   The meeting's going to be earlier than originally planned. They've .... it .... from the 18th to the 15th.

10. The band played the national anthem and everyone in the audience ....

    This is the most comfortable chair, I think. Please, ...

Opposites – 2

As in the previous exercise, complete each pair of sentences by using two phrasal verbs from the list below.

break up	**go back**	**step up**	**cut back**
build up	**die down**	**take down**	**put back**
come on	**go off**	**take off**	**put on**
count in	**count out**	**take off**	**touch down**
start out	**end up**	**talk out of**	**talk into**

1. If the temperature is too low, the heating .... automatically.

   If the temperature is too high, the heating .... automatically .

2. Nowadays Ronald's books are famous all over the world but they .... as stories he told to keep the children amused.

   They were originally children's bedtime stories but they have .... as books, films and even computer games.

3. There was a big increase in orders and we had to .... production.

   There was a sharp decrease in orders so we decided to .... production.

4. You're soaking wet! Now, ... those wet clothes and get into the bath.

   You aren't wearing your slippers! .... them .... or your feet will get cold.

5. Duncan's determined to marry her and you'll never .... him .... it.

   Bob's determined not to sing in the concert and you'll never .... him .... it.

6. The plane .... and soon disappeared behind the clouds.

   The plane .... safely and all the passengers got out.

7. Linda locked the door and .... the cash box .... from the top shelf.

   Linda took some coins out of the box and .... it .... on the shelf.

8. As the audience waited for the star, the excitement .... in the theatre.

   Edwina would only start her speech after the noise had ....

9. Sure! I'd love to help with the show! .... me .... !

   I think it's a crazy idea. I want nothing to do with it! .... me .... !

10. Only a few days of school left. The pupils .... for the holidays next week.

    The vacation will soon be over. The students .... to college on Monday.

Test 1

Choose the correct alternative to complete each sentence.

1. I must go on a diet. I .... a lot of weight while I was on holiday.
    A held up **B** put on **C** settled down **D** weighed up

2. We were .... when we saw how much he had changed.
    A barged in **B** pulled out **C** taken aback **D** whipped up

3. So you've passed your driving test! This .... a celebration!
    A bursts into **B** calls for **C** looks after **D** takes after

4. I try to be friendly but it's hard to .... some of my colleagues.
    A come up with **B** get by **C** get on with **D** speak out

5. I'd better take one of my pills. I think I've got a headache ....
    A catching up **B** coming on **C** dying down **D** winding up

6. The plane .... and was soon flying high over the town.
    A clouded over **B** fired away **C** piled up **D** took off

7. After he was knocked out, it took a long time to ....
    A bring him round **B** fit him in **C** keep him in **D** let him off

8. What do the initials LTP .... ?
    A build up **B** stand for **C** take over **D** turn out

9. As they're identical twins, it's difficult to ....
    A mix them up **B** take them apart **C** tell them apart **D** set them up

10. One of them was injured so the team had to .... the competition.
    A back away from **B** drop out of **C** get back at **D** get behind with

11. That's not the way to solve the problem. You're .... it the wrong way.
    A coming across **B** going about **C** taking over **D** turning on

12. Suddenly the fire alarm .... and everyone had to leave the building.
    A got around **B** set off **C** shot up **D** went off

13. She's so depressed. All these problems are really ....
    A getting her down **B** getting round her **C** taking her on **D** toning her down

14. He .... as a quiet, thoughtful person.
    A bubbles over **B** catches on **C** comes across **D** puts through

15. I'm not going – so don't try to .... me .... going!
    A speak ... to **B** talk ... into **C** tell ... into **D** talk ... out of

16. A car suddenly .... in front of me and I couldn't stop in time.
    A crossed out **B** gave in **C** pulled out **D** shot up

Test 2

Complete each partnership by inserting the missing verb. The list of verbs to choose from is at the bottom of the page but see how many questions you can answer first before you look at the list.

1. .... **on** special make-up when I appear on stage.

2. .... **up** the volume if you can't hear.

3. .... **through** her disguise if she isn't convincing enough.

4. .... **across** these photos while tidying up my room.

5. .... **off** those thin clothes and put on something warmer.

6. .... **back on** the time when we lived in London.

7. .... **through** all that noise while everyone else was woken up.

8. .... **ahead with** all the improvements we've asked for.

9. .... **up** appearances despite all our financial problems.

10. .... **up with** suggestions for places to hold the conference.

11. .... **out in** a rash after eating tomatoes.

12. .... **down** the volume if it's too loud.

13. .... **into** the hotel before the others arrive.

14. .... **forward** a proposal and hope that they'll accept it.

15. .... **up** any new words in a dictionary.

16. .... **into** tears when she heard the news.

17. .... **out on** all the fun if you don't come.

18. .... **away** the secret if they keep questioning him.

Choose from these verbs:

burst   check   come (x3)   give   go   keep   look (x2)
miss   put (x2)   see   sleep   take   turn (x2)

Test 3

Choose the correct alternative to complete each sentence.

1. We heard her .... in agony as she dropped the saucepan on her toe.
   A boil over **B** cry out **C** let off **D** ring out

2. You'll have to .... early if you want to avoid all the traffic.
   A come apart **B** go about **C** put off **D** set off

3. I was so tired that I .... on the sofa and went to sleep.
   A dropped in **B** flaked off **C** glazed over **D** stretched out

4. I had to .... the boss while she was away.
   A move on to **B** put in for **C** stand in for **D** try on

5. We're hoping to .... a reconciliation between the two families.
   A bring about **B** come in for **C** make up **D** take up

6. Some information has .... but we still don't know what exactly is going on.
   A dropped in **B** fallen through **C** got away **D** leaked out

7. The road was blocked so we had to .... and find another route.
   A check out **B** turn back **C** run through **D** fall off

8. Don't worry. The pain should .... fairly soon.
   A break out **B** die out **C** fall off **D** wear off

9. The music .... and it was impossible to have a conversation.
   A blared out **B** played off **C** turned up **D** set out

10. I'm sure he'll .... the chance of earning some extra money!
    A fall for **B** get at **C** jump at **D** stand for

11. We finally managed to .... our point of view.
    A bring her round to **B** fool her into **C** take her up on **D** fix her up with

12. We'll have to .... an extra coach if any more people want to come.
    A settle down **B** pull through **C** lay on **D** stand up for

13. On the day I left, the whole family .... at the station.
    A saw me off **B** showed me out **C** stood in for me **D** took me up

14. Luckily, the rain .... so we were able to play the match.
    A watered down **B** gave out **C** got away **D** held off

15. Why do they .... talking about money all the time?
    A keep on **B** side with **C** take after **D** work off

16. The ceiling .... and several people were trapped.
    A butted in **B** caved in **C** cracked down **D** wore down

110

Test 4

Complete each partnership by inserting the missing verb. The list of verbs to choose from is at the bottom of the page but see how many questions you can answer first before you look at the list.

1. .... **into** a lot of money when her aunt dies.

2. .... **back on** your promise when everyone is depending on you.

3. .... **on** more staff to deal with all the orders.

4. .... **up** the pros and cons before deciding.

5. .... **up against** problems and difficulties.

6. .... **up to** going for a run around the park.

7. .... **up** the bridge with this dynamite.

8. .... **forward to** seeing them again after all this time.

9. .... **off** the meeting to next Tuesday.

10. .... **up** the bank and steal a million pounds.

11. .... **into** decisions instead of taking your time.

12. .... **up** a fuss about the terrible food.

13. .... **you into** a secret if you promise not to tell anyone.

14. .... **in** the application form and then sign it.

15. .... **in for** a lot of criticism because of the way he acted.

16. .... **down** any applicants who look unsuitable.

17. .... **up with** that noise from the lorries going past.

18. .... **into** the army when he leaves school.

Choose from the following verbs:

**blow   come (x3)   feel   fill   go (x2)   hold   kick
let   look   put (x2)   rush   take   turn   weigh**

Test 5

Choose the correct alternative to complete each sentence.

1. How old is he? – He's .... now. He must be at least ninety.
   A coming off **B** getting back **C** getting on **D** falling out

2. So she succeeded in winning the contract. How did she manage to .... ?
   A bring it out **B** pull it off **C** throw it up **D** weigh it up

3. She had to .... because someone else wanted to use the phone.
   A hang up **B** keep up **C** stand out **D** take back

4. The changes were .... gradually so that everyone could get used to them.
   A come to **B** handed over **C** phased in **D** stood in for

5. Violence .... and a lot of people were injured.
   A caught up **B** flared up **C** lifted off **D** turned in

6. A lot of money must have .... that expensive-looking carpet.
   A added up to **B** gambled away **C** gone on **D** got off

7. She was so convincing that we were completely .... by her story.
   A gone through **B** held down **C** taken in **D** told off

8. So many people were ill that we had to .... the meeting.
   A call off **B** mix up **C** set down **D** put out

9. If you need any support, you can rely on me to ....
   A back you up **B** face up to you **C** set you down **D** put you through

10. We .... the old tablecloth on the ground and put the picnic things on it.
    A handed out **B** sewed on **C** screwed up **D** spread out

11. I'll just .... a few details in case I forget something.
    A hand down **B** jot down **C** lapse into **D** look forward to

12. The meeting .... and I got more and more bored.
    A dragged on **B** ebbed away **C** fell off **D** switched off

13. Your name .... in the course of conversation.
    A came up **B** kept on **C** set out **D** turned out

14. They were so angry at his speech that they .... in protest.
    A fell through **B** signed away **C** warmed up **D** walked out

15. I had to .... and admit I had made a mistake.
    A climb down **B** fall down **C** let out **D** tighten up

16. It was supposed to be a private meeting but he just .... !
    A barged in **B** broke off **C** crowded around **D** whiled away

Mini-Dictionary

The verbs are listed in the order in which they first appear. Where 3 dots (...) are used, this means that the object must go in this position.

account for ... – explain
How do you account for their strange behaviour?

accuse ... – of say that someone has committed a crime
He was accused of stealing the money.

act on ... – take action as the result of (eg advice)
We acted on your advice and took the early train.

add on ... – include in your calculations
Don't forget to add on some money for expenses.

add up to ... – result in a total of
The money owed added up to over two thousand pounds.

aim at ... – try to affect or influence certain people
This advertisement is obviously aimed at teenagers.

answer to (a description) – correspond to a description
The man we arrested answered to the crimnal's description.

approve of ... – think something is good
I don't approve of all this loud modern music.

ask for ... – make something likely to happen
You'll be asking for trouble if you criticise her work.

ask in – ask someone to come in
Don't leave your friend on the doorstep. Ask him in!

ask out – ask someone to go out with you
I asked Sharon out but she said she had lots of homework to do.

back away – retreat, move backwards
The bank staff backed away as the gunman came nearer.

back away from ... – retreat from
The postman backed away from the angry dog.

back down – no longer keep to your position in an argument
Neither party wanted to back down so the argument continued.

back out – not do as promised
The pianist has backed out so I've got to find another one.

back out of ... – withdraw from (eg an agreement)
I'll back out of the agreement unless things improve.

back up – give someone help and support
My friends backed me up when I complained about the noise.

back up – make a copy of work on a computer
I always back up my work in case something happens.

bail out – (of a pilot) jump out of an aeroplane in flight
The pilot managed to bail out just before the plane crashed.

barge in – rush in rudely, interrupt
Sheila barged in just as the conversation was getting interesting.

batter down – keep hitting something until it falls to the ground
The firemen had to batter down the door to get in.

be away – have gone somewhere else
Our head of department's away on a business trip.

be down – feel depressed
He's been down ever since his dog died.

be down – have fallen, decreased
Unfortunately, profits are down by 20 per cent.

be down with ... – have caught some kind of illness
Barry can't come to the meeting. He's down with a virus.

be in – arrive
Competition entries must be in by the end of the week.

be in – have come into fashion
That hairstyle is definitely in at the moment.

be in – be at home
She should be in from work soon.

be in – (of the tide) be high
When the tide is in, there isn't much room on the beach.

be in on ... – be involved in something
I don't know much about it as I wasn't in on the planning.

be off – start a journey
When are you off? - At six o'clock tomorrow evening.

be off – (of food) have gone bad
Smell this cream. I think it's off.

be on – be taking place
The play is on for another three nights.

be on – be working, have been switched on
There must be someone inside. The television is on.

be out – not be at home, have left a building temporarily
The boss is out at the moment but he'll be back soon.

be out of ... – no longer have any left
I'm afraid we're out of sugar at the moment.

be up – have risen
Profits are up by fifty per cent.

be up – have got out of bed to start the day
Gerry's so lazy! It's eleven o'clock and she still isn't up yet!

be up – (of time) have expired
Time's up. Please stop writing.

be up to – be doing (usually something wrong)
You're looking guilty. What have you been up to?

beat down – (of the sun) shine and be extremely hot
It was midday and the sun was beating down.

beat up – hit or kick someone and hurt them badly
The thieves beat the victim up and stole all his money.

bed down – sleep somewhere unusual
We had to bed down in the stables for the night.

belong to ... – be owned by
That yacht must belong to someone really rich.

bend down – move the top of the body downwards
He bent down and picked up a piece of paper.

black out – stop the lights working (n. blackout)
The power cut blacked out half the city.

blare out (of music) – be very loud
The music blared out and gave me a terrible headache.

blaze away (of a fire) – burn fiercely
The fire blazed away and soon warmed us up.

blaze away – shoot rapidly and continuously
The terrorists blazed away with their machine guns.

blow down (of wind) – cause to fall down
The trees were blown down by the fierce wind.

blow out – extinguish (eg a candle) by blowing
Mother blew out the candle and the room went dark.

blow over (of a storm) – pass
The storm finally blew over early this morning.

blow up – destroy with an explosion
We'll need more explosives to blow up the bridge.

boil over (of a liquid) – boil and go over the top of a pan
The milk boiled over and left a terrible mess.

book up – reserve a seat (eg for the theatre)
The show was booked up weeks before it opened.

boss around – keep telling someone what to do
I know what I'm doing! Stop bossing me around!

bottle up (feelings) – suppress feelings
I was very angry but I tried to bottle up my feelings.

bottom out – reach the lowest point
The recession bottomed out and things began to improve.

branch out – develop in new areas
This firm should branch out and develop different products.

break away – separate from a political party (adj. breakaway)
Some dissidents broke away and formed their own party.

break down – stop working
My car broke down at the traffic lights.

break down – lose control of your emotions (n. breakdown)
My aunt broke down when she heard the awful news.

break down – keep hitting something until it falls to the ground
We had to break down the door to get in.

break in – enter, using force
The firemen broke in and rescued the children from the house.

break in – interrupt a conversation
Could I just break in there and make a comment?

break in – enter a building in order to steal something
The thieves broke in and stole all her jewellery.

break in (an animal) – tame an animal
It takes patience to break in wild horses.

break in on ... – interrupt (eg a conversation)
I hate to break in on their conversation, but it's time to go.

break into ... – enter in order to steal something
The thief broke into the office and stole the plans.

break off – end, discontinue (eg a relationship)
Tanya broke off their relationship when she went to college.

break off – separate something by breaking
My friend broke off a piece of chocolate and gave me some.

break out – escape from prison
The prisoners broke out during a rest period.

break out (of fighting) – start (n. outbreak)
Fighting has broken out and many people have been injured.

break out of ... – escape from (eg prison)
You'll never break out of this prison. It's too well guarded.

break through ... – penetrate using force
The crowd broke through the barriers and onto the pitch.

break up (of a party, meeting) – end
The party finally broke up at midnight.

break up – start a school holiday
The children break up for the summer holiday next week.

break up – break into pieces, disintegrate
The storm was so severe that the ship broke up on the rocks.

breathe out – exhale
Hold your breath and then breathe out slowly.

bring about – cause to happen
What brought about this change in attitude?

bring along – bring someone with you
If Sue's interested, why not bring her along to the next meeting?

bring back (memories) – make you think about a past event
This place brings back memories of my childhood.

bring back – return something
My neighbour's just brought back the tools he borrowed.

bring down (the government) – cause it to lose power
The opposition parties conspired to bring down the government.

bring down (prices) – reduce prices
We hope to get more customers by reducing prices.

bring down – cause to fall to the ground
Our centre forward was brought down by one of their defenders.

bring forward – arrange to have (eg a meeting) earlier
They've brought the meeting forward to this Saturday.

bring in (money) – earn money
The job brings in an extra hundred pounds a week.

bring in (a verdict) – reach a verdict
The jury brought in a verdict of not guilty.

bring in – arrest and bring to a police station
Let's bring her in for questioning about the robbery

bring ... in on – involve in a discussion etc
Let's bring Bill in on our discussion.

bring on – cause, lead to
All the exertion brought on an attack of asthma.

bring on – train, develop
We try to bring on any promising athletes.

bring out (a product) – introduce a product on to the market
We're bringing out several new models next year.

bring ... out in – cause (eg a rash) to appear on the body
Eating strawberries brings Muriel out in a rash.

bring ... round – bring back to consciousness
They tried to bring Brian round after he had fainted.

bring ... round – to persuade someone to agree with you.
You'll never bring her round to your point of view.

bring up – look after and educate (a child) (n. upbringing)
I was brought up by my grandparents from the age of five.

bring up – mention
Did the manager bring up the question of finance again?

bring up – bring something upstairs
Could you bring up a glass of water when you come to bed?

bristle (with anger) – look very angry
She bristled with anger when she saw the damage.

brush off – brush something until it comes off a surface
Can you brush the dirt off the back of my jacket?

brush up – improve your knowledge and skill
I went on a course to brush up my Spanish.

bubble over – be full of (excitement etc)
We were bubbling over with excitement as we got on the coach.

build up – get (your strength and health) back after an illness
After my illness, I had to do exercises to build up my strength.

build up a business – develop a business
He has built this business up into a multi-national company.

build up – increase (n. build-up)
If the gas keeps building up there will be an explosion.

build up – cover an area in buildings (adj. built-up)
They've really built up this area. All the trees have gone.

bump into ... – meet by chance
I bumped into an old friend in town yesterday.

burn down – be completely destroyed by fire
I rescued a few possessions before the house burned down.

burst into (applause) – suddenly start applauding
The audience burst into applause when the star appeared.

burst into (tears) – begin (crying) suddenly
Wilma burst into tears when I told her that her cat had died.

burst into (flames) – suddenly start burning
I was cooking with the frying pan when it burst into flames.

burst out (laughing) – suddenly start (eg laughing) (n. outburst)
The crowd burst out laughing at the clown.

butt in – take part in a conversation without being asked
Can I just butt in here and make a point?

call ... after – give the same name as
She was called Elizabeth, after her grandmother.

call for ... – require
This situation calls for urgent action.

call for ... – go (to a building) and collect someone
My boyfriend's calling for me at half past six.

call for ... – demand
People are calling for an inquiry into the accident.

call in – ask (an expert) to come and do something for you
We'll have to call in a plumber to fix that leak.

call in – stop at a place while on the way to somewhere else
I called in on the way home to see how they were.

call in – ask for something to be returned because of a problem
The manufacturer called in those cars to check the brakes.

call off – cancel
They called off the match because the weather was so bad.

call on ... – ask, appeal to
I call on you all for your help.

call on ... – visit
Shall we call on your sister when we go to London?

call out – contact someone and ask them to come and help
When the fire got serious, we called out the fire brigade.

call out – speak in a loud voice
When I call out your name, I want you to step forward.

call out – tell workers to go on strike
When negotiations broke down, we were called out on strike.

call up – phone
I would have called you up but I didn't know your number.

calm down – stop being angry
Calm down! Think of your blood pressure!

camp out – sleep outside in a tent
My daughter wants to camp out in the tent tonight.

carried away – filled with emotion so that you lose control
We were carried away by the rhythm of the music.

carry off (a prize) – win a prize
Alexa is so good that she's certain to carry off first prize.

carry on ... – continue
The secretaries carried on working as if nothing had happened.

carry on with ... – continue (an activity)
Don't let me disturb you. Carry on with what you're doing.

carry out – conduct, perform (eg a survey)
We're carrying out a survey into people's eating habits.

carry out – do (as instructed, as you have threatened etc)
The soldiers carried out their threat and attacked the town.

catch on – become popular
I don't think this new hairstyle will really catch on.

catch on – realise what is happening
Douglas finally caught on and realised it was all a joke.

catch up – get to the same standard as the others
I've missed some lessons and I need to catch up.

catch up on ... – do work which should already have been done
You've got all that homework to catch up on.

catch up with ... – get to the same level
I had to work hard to catch up with the rest of the class.

cave in (of a ceiling) – collapse
The roof leaked and the water caused the ceiling to cave in.

change over – change to a new system (n. change-over)
We changed over to the new filing system last year.

charge ... with – formally accuse of
The man we'd arrested was charged with burglary.

check in – register at a hotel or airport (n. check-in)
If you check in early, you'll be sure of a window seat.

check into ... – register at a hotel or airport
We finally checked into our hotel at ten o'clock.

check out (of a hotel) – pay the bill and leave a hotel
We have to check out by eleven at the latest.

cheer on – encourage by cheering
The crowd cheered the runner on as he struggled to finish.

cheer up – become less miserable
Cheer up! Things can't be that bad!

chop down – cut (eg a tree) with an axe until it falls to the ground
The tree was diseased so we had to chop it down.

clean out – remove unwanted articles and clean thoroughly
I found these books while I was cleaning out the cupboard.

clean up – clean thoroughly (n. clean-up)
This room is a mess! When are you going to clean it up?

clear away – remove things you have been using
Please clear away your books so I can lay the table.

clear off – go away (impolite)
Clear off! We don't want people like you around here!

clear out – tidy and throw away things no longer needed
I'm going to clear out my cupboard to make more storage space.

clear up – tidy, put in order
We'll have to clear up this mess before the vistors arrive.

clear up (of an infection) – disappear
The antibiotics will help the infection to clear up.

climb down – admit you were wrong
Her boss had to climb down and admit he had misjudged her.

close down – close permanently
If business doesn't improve, we'll have to close down a factory.

cloud over (of the sky) – be covered in clouds
It's clouding over. It looks as if it's going to rain.

come across ... – find by chance
I was lucky. I came across this vase in a second-hand shop.

come across – give the impression of being
The new teacher comes across as a very nervous person.

come apart – break into pieces
This model just came apart when I picked it up.

come before ... – come to a court and face (eg a judge)
When you come before the judge, I advise you to plead guilty.

come down (of rain etc) – fall
The children sat by the window, watching the rain coming down.

come down – come from the north, or from the town to the country
Why don't you come down and see us some time?

come down – reach a decision
The committee of enquiry came down against the motorway.

come down on ... – criticise severely
The porter came down on me like a ton of bricks for losing the key.

come forward with ... – give ideas or information
We want the public to come forward with any information.

come from ... – have as your country or place of origin
I come from Perth, in Australia.

come in (useful) – prove to be useful
This box might come in useful one day.

come in (of news) – be received
News has just come in of a fire at Heathrow Airport.

come in ... – be placed in a race
Unfortunately, I came in last in the race.

come in (of a flight) – arrive at an airport (adj. incoming)
Our relatives' flight finally came in ten hours late.

come in (for criticism) – be criticised
Her new TV programme has come in for a lot of criticism.

come in – (of the tide) be high
This beach is completely covered when the tide comes in.

come into ... – inherit
Darren will come into a lot of money when his grandfather dies.

come into use – start being used
The new system came into use last month.

come into ... – be relevant
Money doesn't come into it. It's not at all important.

come off – become unstuck
The poster came off so I had to stick it on again.

come off (of players) – leave the place where a game is being played
The match was stopped and the players had to come off.

Come off it! – "I don't believe you!"
Come off it! He's at least fifty! Don't talk such rubbish!

come on (of an illness) – start
I think I've got a cold coming on.

come on – an expression used to encourage someone
Come on! Don't be frightened! You can do it!

come on (of electrical equipment) – start
The heating comes on at five in the morning.

come on – appear on the stage
I only come on at the end of the play.

come out (of a stain) – disappear
This stuff should make the stain come out.

come out (of a secret) – be revealed
When the story of his secret life came out we were all shocked.

come out (of a book or film) – be available to the public
His new film comes out next month.

come out (of the sun) – appear in the sky
The clouds went away and the sun came out.

come out – leave a room or building
The school bell rang and all the pupils came out.

come out in ... – have (eg spots) on your body
I came out in a terrible rash after eating those berries.

come out with ... – come with other people to the cinema etc
Sandra's got some work so she can't come out with us tonight.

come over ... – affect
I suddenly started trembling. I don't know what came over me.

come round – regain consciousness
She took ages to come round after she'd fainted.

come through (of a message) – arrive
A message has just come through from headquarters.

come to ... – be necessary, be a question of
When it comes to doing the ironing, I'm hopeless.

come to – recover consciousness
I was in a coma for ten days when I finally came to.

come up (of the sun) – rise
We left early in the morning as the sun was coming up.

come up – come near to
A man came up and asked the way to the station.

come up – be mentioned
Your name came up in the course of conversation.

come up – arise, appear
An opportunity for extra work has come up.

come up against ... – be faced by
We came up against many problems when we built our house.

come up to expectations – reach the level expected
Unfortunately, the holiday didn't come up to expectations.

come up with ... – think of (eg a solution)
Even the experts can't come up with the answer to our problem.

confuse ... with – not be able to tell the difference
You're confusing me with my brother, who's also a doctor.

cool down – become cooler
The soup's too hot. I'll leave it to cool down.

coop up – keep in a confined place
The prisoners are cooped up in their cells for 23 hours a day.

copy down – write a copy of
Please copy down what I've written on the board.

cordon off – erect barriers to restrict movement
The police cordoned off the area to prevent any incidents.

count ... in – include, involve in an activity
Sure, count me in. I'd love to help.

count on ... – rely on
I hope I can count on you to be there on time.

count ... out – exclude from an activity
You can count me out. I'm much too old to go to disco-dancing.

crack down – act more strictly
The police are cracking down to prevent any more trouble.

crack up – have a nervous breakdown
You'll crack up if you keep working so hard.

crop up – appear, happen unexpectedly
A problem has cropped up so I may be working all night.

cross out – put a line through (eg a mistake)
I need a ruler to cross out this mistake.

crowd around ... – surround in large numbers
Everyone crowded around her and tried to get her autograph.

crowd into ... – go into a place in large numbers
Thousands of people crowded into the stadium.

cry out – make a loud noise of pain, fear etc
We heard him cry out in pain as the ball hit his arm.

cut back – reduce
They had to cut back production during the recession.

cut back on – reduce
We'll have to cut back on luxuries if my salary goes down.

cut down – consume less
You eat too many sweets. You should try to cut down.

cut down on ... – reduce
Try to cut down on the amount of fat you eat every day.

cut ... down (to size) – reduce the importance of
His uniform didn't impress. They soon cut him down to size.

cut off – disconnect a phone call
I was cut off in the middle of an important phone call.

cut off – separate and isolate
The snow fell all night and cut off the town.

cut off – separate by cutting (adj. cut-off)
Alexa cut off the bottoms of her jeans and made them into shorts.

cut out – not include
I'm trying to cut out any desserts with a high sugar content.

cut out (of an engine) – suddenly stop working
The engine suddenly cut out and I couldn't start it again.

cut it out – stop being unreasonable
Oh, cut it out! Don't be so silly!

cut up (adj.) – upset
He was very cut up when his dog died.

dawn on ... – become clear to
It finally dawned on me that I'd made a terrible mistake.

deal with ... – do something about
The manager will deal with any complaints.

deal with ... – (of a newspaper article etc) be about
The article deals with the problems of getting old.

deal with ... – do business with
We deal with many foreign companies.

die away (of a noise) – become weaker, fainter
The noise of the band died away and the crowd dispersed.

die down – decrease, become quieter
When the noise had died down, the chairman went on speaking.

die out (of a tradition) – disappear
Many traditional crafts have died out in the last fifty years.

dig into ... – put your hand inside something and look for something
The security guard dug into his pocket and took out a key.

dig up – discover hidden information
The reporters were trying to dig up information about her.

disagree with ... – (of food or drink) make you feel ill
I don't eat onions. They disagree with me.

dispose of ... – get rid of
We must find a safe way of disposing of all these chemicals.

do away with ... – abolish
They've done away with the old system of enrolling for courses.

do up – fasten
Do up your coat or you'll catch cold!

do up – decorate, make repairs to
I'll need some more paint as I'm going to do up this room.

could do with ... – need
I'm thirsty. I could do with a long, cool drink.

doze off – fall into a light sleep
It was so warm that I must have dozed off for a moment.

drag on – continue unnecessarily for a long time
The meeting dragged on until 11 o'clock at night!

draw up (of a vehicle) – come to a place and stop
The car drew up and the driver opened his door.

draw up – prepare (eg a contract)
We'll draw up the contract and send you a copy to look at.

draw up – pull something close to something else
The doctor drew up a chair next to the bed.

wouldn't dream of ... – wouldn't consider
I wouldn't dream of wearing such a terrible dress!

dream up – think of (a new activity etc)
I have to keep dreaming up new activities to keep them amused.

dress up – put on smart, elegant or formal clothes
It's a formal wedding so we'll have to dress up.

drink to ... – drink and hope for success
Let's drink to success in the competition.

drink up – finish your drink
It's time to drink up and go.

drive off – leave in a vehicle
One customer drove off without paying for the petrol.

drop away – get smaller in number, become less strong
Support dropped away as he failed to keep his promises.

drop in – visit casually
I just dropped in to see if anyone wanted to go swimming.

drop out – withdraw (eg from a competition)
Two competitors have dropped out because of injury.

drop out – leave, not complete (eg a college course) (n. drop-out)
Some students drop out when the course gets more difficult.

drop out of ... – stop belonging to (eg a college)
After she dropped out of college, she worked as a waitress.

dry up – come to an end
If supplies of petrol dry up, our cars will be useless.

ease off – become less intense
When the rain eases off, I'll go and do my shopping.

eat out – go out and have a meal
I'm tired of cooking. Let's eat out tonight.

eat up – eat all the food you are given
Eat up all your vegetables. They're full of vitamins.

end up – eventually become (something not originally planned)
Michael started off as an actor but ended up as a TV announcer.

enter for ... – put your name down as a competitor
I've decided to enter for the Glamorous Grandmother contest.

evict ... **from** – force to leave
Aaron couldn't pay the rent so he was evicted from the flat.

face up to ... – accept and deal with a difficulty
You'll have to face up to the problem some time.

fall back – retreat
The enemy fire was so intense that the troops had to fall back.

fall down – fall to the ground
The girl on the roof slipped and fell down.

fall down (of an argument) – be weak
That argument falls down when you take the cost into account.

fall for ... – be deceived by
How could I have fallen for that old trick?

fall for ... – be strongly attracted to, fall in love with
Byron always falls for women with long red hair.

fall in (of a ceiling or roof) – collapse
The ceiling fell in and several people were badly injured.

fall off – fall from where it was placed on to the floor
I knocked the table and a glass fell off.

fall off – decrease
Membership has fallen off since they put up the prices.

fall out – quarrel, no longer be friends
They fell out over a loan and haven't spoken since then.

fall out (of hair) – come away from the head
If my hair keeps falling out at this rate, I'll soon be bald.

fall through (of a plan) – not succeed
Unfortunately, the plan fell through so we still haven't met her.

feel up to ... – feel capable, well enough to do something
I'm too tired. I don't feel up to jogging today.

fence off – separate by erecting a fence
We'll fence off this area and build a playground.

fight off – repel, not allow to come near
The old lady tried to fight off the wolf with a stick.

file away – put away in a file
Please file away this report.

fill in – give all the information to someone
You obviously don't know what's happened so I'll fill you in.

fill in – complete (a form)
Make sure you fill in the form correctly.

fill in – take someone's place and do their work
I'm filling in while the manager's away.

fill ... **in on** – give someone all the information about
I'd better fill you in on the details of what happened.

fill up – make full
I'll fill up the tank with petrol before we leave.

fill ... **(with confidence)** – make someone very confident
The coach's talk filled the team with confidence.

filter out – get rid of something unwanted (eg noise, an impurity)
These ear-plugs should filter out most of the noise.

find out – discover
Did you find out where he lives?

fire away – begin asking questions
I've got a few more questions. - All right. Fire away.

fish for ... – try to get (information etc) in an indirect way
He was around here again, fishing for information.

fit in – be contained in the space provided
All this luggage won't fit in. The boot's too small.

fit in – work well with others in a group
I just didn't fit in well with the rest of the group.

fit in – have enough time for an activity
I might be able to fit in a short meeting tomorrow afternoon.

fix ... **up with** – arrange for someone to have (eg a job)
He's fixed me up with a job at the local supermarket.

flake off (of paint) – come off in flakes
The paint began to flake off in the sunshine.

flare up (of violence) – suddenly start and become serious
Violence flared up after a man was killed in a fight.

fling (yourself) into ... – start doing something enthusiastically
She flung herself into her work with great enthusiasm.

flood in – come in large numbers
Applications came flooding in from all over the country.

flutter down – come down to the ground like a leaf
The pieces of paper fluttered down to the street below.

fly into ... – suddenly get very angry etc
She flew into a rage when she saw the mess they had made.

fold up – make neat by folding
He folded up the document and put it carefully away.

fool around with ... – behave in a careless or irresponsible way
You shouldn't let children fool around with matches.

fool ... **into** deceive someone and make them do something
He fooled them into believing he was a policeman.

freeze over (of a stretch of water) – be covered in ice
Last winter the lake froze over.

freeze up – be covered in ice
It was so cold that the pipes froze up.

freshen up – wash and make yourself look more presentable
The bathroom's upstairs if you'd like to freshen up.

gamble (money) away – lose money by gambling
He gambled away all the money he had inherited.

get a message across – communicate, make people understand
It wasn't easy to get my message across in such a short time.

get around (of news) – be known everywhere
The news of the robbery soon got around.

get at ... – discover (the truth etc)
I wonder if we'll ever get at the truth of his disappearance?

get at ... – reach, find
That light is too high for me to get at.

get at ... – criticise
Mr Grouch is always getting at me, even when it's not my fault.

get away – escape (n. getaway)
The thieves got away in a stolen car.

get away – go away on holiday
We hope to get away for a holiday in the country.

Get away! – "I don't believe you!"
Norma's a millionaire, you know. - Get away! You're joking!

get away with ... – escape, not get caught
The thieves managed to get away with most of her jewellery.

get away with ... – receive a relatively light punishment
As it was her first offence, Sandy got away with only a fine.

get (your breath) back – stop feeling out of breath
I had to stop running to get my breath back.

get back – return from a journey
The family got back home in the early evening.

get back – be given back something you have lent
I've finally got back those books I lent her.

get back – move away
Get back! You're standing too close!

get back at ... – get revenge on
Edna's got back at the men who ruined her business.

get behind with ... – be late in paying
If you get behind with the rent, you might lose the flat.

get by – just manage financially
It's difficult to get by on my salary.

get by – get past
He stood in the way and we couldn't get by.

get down – climb down from a high place
Louis fell as he was getting down from the tree.

get ... down – annoy, make unhappy
This cold weather is really getting me down.

get down – write, make a note of
The clerk spoke slowly so that I could get down all the details.

get down to ... – start (some work)
That's enough talking. Let's get down to some work.

get in – enter (a building etc)
The thief got in through the window.

get in – arrive home
By the time I got in they'd already had dinner.

get in (of a train etc) – arrive at its destination
The train should get in at seven thirty.

get in – do (some practice etc)
We must get in some more practice before the big match.

get in – bring indoors
It's raining. Shall I help you get the washing in?

get in – ask (an electrician etc) to come and repair something
I don't understand this wiring. I'll have to get in an electrician.

get into ... – be involved in an unpleasant situation (eg trouble, debt)
They were forced to sell their house when they got into debt.

get into (clothes) – put on clothes, often with difficulty
I'm larger now and I can't get into my old clothes.

get off – leave (a bus, train etc)
Get off at the stop after the town hall.

get off – not be convicted of a crime
Morris might get off if the judge believes his story.

get off (to sleep) – start sleeping
It took me ages to get off to sleep last night.

tell ... where to get off – criticise someone for their behaviour
The doorman was so rude that I told him where to get off.

get on – have a good relationship
Tracey and I have always got on really well.

get on – become old
I'm getting on, you know. I'm nearly seventy.

get on – continue an activity
I must get on or I'll never finish this letter.

get on ... – get into (a bus etc)
The bus was full so we couldn't get on.

get on – progress
How are you getting on in your new job?

get on (like a house on fire) – be great friends
They've only just met but they're getting on like a house on fire.

get on with ... – have a good relationship with
Trish is very pleasant and easy to get on with.

get on with ... – continue with an activity
Please stop talking and get on with your work!

get out – escape from a building
The boys managed to get out by climbing through a window.

get out – leave a car or building
The car stopped and the driver got out.

get out of ... – avoid doing something
I managed to get out of doing the washing up.

get over – communicate, make people understand
It was difficult to get my message over in a simple way.

get over ... – recover from
You need rest to help you get over your operation.

get ... over with – finish doing something unpleasant
Let's get this horrible test over with and then we can relax.

get round ... – persuade someone to change their mind
Judy got round him somehow to lend her his car.

get round to ... – finally do something after a long delay
I've finally got round to answering my uncle's letter.

get through to ... – contact (eg by phone)
All the lines are engaged. I can't get through to head office.

get to ... – annoy
Calm down! Don't let his sarcasm get to you.

get together – assemble (n. get-together)
We get together once a year to talk about old times.

get up – leave your bed and start the day
The alarm rang but I had difficulty getting up.

get up ... – get to the top of
It took me ten minutes to get up that hill!

get up – organise
They've got up a petition to protest against the tax increases.

get up to ... – do (usually something naughty)
I'm sure those children are getting up to some mischief.

give away (a secret) – reveal a secret
I'll tell you as long as you promise not to give away my secret.

give away – give without expecting payment
They're giving away free samples of the new chocolate bar.

give back – return something borrowed
When is Heather going to give back the ladder she borrowed?

give in – stop making an effort
You've nearly finished. Don't give in now.

give in – give somebody some work you have done
Please give in your homework by Monday.

give off ... – emit (eg a smell)
The mixture was giving off a strange smell.

give out – distribute
Can you give out these books as the people arrive?

give out ... – emit (eg heat, fumes)
The factory chimney was giving out black clouds of smoke.

give out – stop working because of tiredness or overuse
After all these years the drinks machine has finally given out.

give up – stop permanently
Since I gave up smoking my cough has gone.

give up (time) – spend time
I give up some of my time to help run the local youth club.

give up – abandon, end (eg a search)
The police had to give up the search when it got dark.

give up – allow someone to sit, stand in (your seat)
I gave up my seat to the old lady and stood.

give ... up (as a bad job) – stop because it seems pointless
I kept trying to phone but in the end I gave it up as a bad job.

glaze over (of eyes) – lose all their expression
The patient's eyes glazed over and he started breathing heavily.

go about ... – deal with, tackle (a task)
How do you go about getting rats out of your garden?

go after ... – try to get (eg a job)
I've decided to go after that job as a receptionist.

go after ... – chase
It's no use going after the thieves. You'll never catch them.

go against (of a verdict) – be unfavourable
If the verdict goes against me, I'll lose my home.

go ahead – proceed, do what you want to do (n. go-ahead)
Dad said we could go ahead and build a tree-house.

go ahead with ... – proceed with
We now intend to go ahead with the final stage of the project.

go along with (a suggestion) – agree to a suggestion
Let's have a pizza. - I'll go along with that.

go away – leave a place
I do not want to buy anything! Please go away!

go back on a promise – not keep a promise
Grandma said she'd come but she went back on her promise.

go by (of time) – pass
As time went by, Graham grew more fond of her.

go by – use for guidance
Don't go by my watch. It's fast.

go by – pass, go past
We stood in the front garden and watched the parade go by.

go down (of the sun) – set
The two of them stood hand in hand, watching the sun go down.

go down (of news) – be received
The news of the dismissals didn't go down very well.

go down – get smaller, decrease
I can put my shoe on again - the swelling has gone down.

go down on your knees – kneel down or apologize
You should go down on your knees and apologise!

go down with ... – catch some kind of disease
Viv's gone down with flu so she won't be in the office today.

go for ... – choose
I expect the council will go for the cheaper option.

go for ... – attack
My wife suddenly turned and went for me with the kitchen knife.

go for ... – find attractive
Helen usually goes for men who dress well.

go in (of the sun) – go behind a cloud
The sun went in and it started to feel cold.

go in – enter hospital as a patient
I'm going in for my operation on Tuesday.

go in ... – fit inside
These clothes won't all go in my suitcase.

go in for (a competition) – enter a competition
Let's go in for the swimming competition.

go into ... – start some kind of employment as a career
When Charles was eighteen he went into the army.

go into ... – talk about in detail
They wouldn't go into what happened in much detail.

go into (hospital) – enter hospital as a patient
Betty's gone into hospital for a minor operation.

go off – become bad
Smell this cheese. I think it's gone off.

go off ... – begin to dislike
She went off him when he started smoking.

go off (of an alarm) – suddenly make a noise
The fire alarm went off and we all rushed out.

go off (of electrical equipment) – stop
The heating goes off automatically at midnight.

go off (at the deep end) – become very angry
When Steve saw the damage, he went off at the deep end.

go on – continue
Shall I go on or have you heard enough?

go on – be guided by
The police haven't got much information to go on.

go on – happen
What's going on outside?

go on ... – be spent on
Most of our money goes on food and clothes.

go on (of electrical equipment) – start working
The heating goes on automatically if it gets too cold.

go on about ... – continually talk about
I wish Diane wouldn't go on about her boyfriend all the time.

go on with ... – continue doing
Please go on with your work. Don't let me stop you.

go out – leave your home to go to the cinema etc
Sorry, I'm going out this evening. What about tomorrow?

go out (of the tide) – go away from the shore
The tide goes out a long way on this part of the coast.

go out (of a light) – stop giving out light
There was a power cut and all the lights went out.

go out (like a light) – become unconscious
He hit me and I went out like a light.

go out with ... – go with someone to the cinema etc
If Trevor asked you, would you go out with him?

go through – be completed successfully
After a lot of discussion the deal finally went through.

go through ... – experience
I hope I never go through an experience like that again!

go through ... – examine, review
I'll go through my notes once more just before the exam.

go through (a procedure) – perform a procedure
You go through a complicated procedure to start the machine.

go through with ... – complete something you agreed to do
Dan's promised to marry her, but will he go through with it?

go under (of a company) – fail, go bankrupt
If we can't get the loan, the company will go under.

go up – rise
Prices have gone up by five per cent this year.

go up – start to burn
The crowd stood and watched the building go up in flames.

go up (of a cheer) – be heard
A cheer went up as the champion appeared.

go up – approach
We went up and asked her if she was all right.

go with ... – combine well with
I need a brown handbag to go with the jacket.

go without ... – not have
I had to go without sugar because I'd forgotten to buy some.

grow into – become large enough to wear properly
Grant will soon grow into that jacket.

grow out of ... – no longer behave in the same way
It's an annoying habit but she should grow out of it.

119

grow up – change from child to adult
I was born and grew up in a tiny village.
hand down – give to the next generation
This necklace has been handed down from mother to daughter.
hand in – give someone some work you have done
Please hand in last night's homework.
hand in (your notice) – resign from your job
She handed in her notice when she found a better job.
hand out – distribute
Can you hand out these books to all the people here?
hand over – give to someone else (n. hand-over)
Mr Bly's handed over the running of the company to me.
hand it to ... – admire someone
You've got to hand it to Louise. She could sell anything.
hang around ... – stay in a place doing nothing in particular
Those boys were still hanging around the entrance when I left.
hang up – end a phone conversation
I'd better hang up as someone wants to use the phone.
head for ... – move in the direction of
We were so hungry that we headed for the nearest restaurant.
heal over (of a wound) – close and become healthy
When the wound has healed over you can remove the plaster.
heal up – become healthy and normal again
How long will it take for this cut to heal up?
hear from ... – receive a letter or phone call from
I haven't heard from Mandy since she wrote in July.
hear of ... – get news of
Let me know if you hear of any vacancies.
help yourself to – serve yourself with
Please help yourself to salad.
hit it off – become friends
Bill and Ted have so much in common. They're sure to hit it off.
hit on ... – suddenly think of
We've just hit on a new slogan for the advert.
hold ... against – allow something to give you a bad impression
John always looks miserable but don't hold it against him.
hold back – restrain, not show (eg tears)
It was difficult to hold back the tears.
hold back (information) – not give, reveal information
If you hold back information, you could be arrested.
hold down – restrain, not allow to get up
Hold the animal down while I give it an injection.
hold down (a job) – keep a job
He's so lazy that he has difficulty holding down a job.
hold down (prices) – not increase prices
We held down our prices while others increased theirs.
hold off (of weather) – not occur as expected, be delayed
Luckily the rain held off until the match was over.
hold on – wait
Hold on a moment. I'll see if she's in.
hold up – use the threat of violence to rob (n. hold-up)
That's the second time the bank's been held up this year.
hold up – keep something up in position
Use some stronger pieces of wood to hold up the shelves.
hold up – delay, stop moving
The traffic was held up because of an accident.
hope for ... – want something to happen
We're all hoping for better weather during our holiday.
hot up (of competition) – intensify, become fiercer
Competition is hotting up and someone's going to get hurt.
hurry up – do things faster
If you don't hurry up, we'll miss the plane.
ice over (of water) – become covered in ice
The pond iced over, causing problems for the ducks.

ice up – become covered in ice
The wings of the plane iced up and the pilot lost control.
identify with ... – be similar to and feel sympathy for
The same thing happened to me. I can identify with her problem.
inform on – betray, give harmful information about
One of the gang informed on their leader and he was arrested.
invite in – ask someone to come into your house
Why don't you invite them in for a cup of tea?
invite out – ask someone to go out
Lynda's invited me out to the theatre this evening.
join in – become involved in an activity with other people
They were going to play football and wanted me to join in.
jot down – make a note of information
I'll just jot down your name and address.
jump at (an opportunity) – seize an opportunity enthusiastically
I thought Jessie would jump at the chance of a free holiday.
jump on ... – jump and get on something
Lloyd jumped on the bus just as it was leaving.
jump out – come out quickly and suddenly
As Pat was passing the doorway, a man jumped out.
jump up – stand up suddenly
The pupils all jumped up as the teacher entered the room.
keep at it – continue doing something (despite difficulties)
I know your homework is difficult but you must keep at it.
keep away – not allow to come near
This spray should keep away mosquitoes.
keep back (information) – not tell, reveal information
Did he tell you everything? - Isn't he keeping something back.
keep down – stay in a low position
Keep down or the soldier will see you.
keep down – keep at a low level
If we keep prices down, we won't lose customers.
keep down – control, restrict the freedom of
The dictator used his army to keep the people down.
keep in – not allow to leave as a punishment
The teacher kept them in after class for being noisy.
keep in – keep to the side of the road
Keep well in as you walk down country roads.
keep ... from – prevent someone from doing something
I tried to keep my dog from chasing the cat.
keep off (a subject) – not mention a subject
Keep off the subject of holidays as she can't afford one this year.
keep off ... – not walk on
Please keep off the grass.
keep off (of rain or snow) – not start
Luckily, the rain kept off until the evening.
keep off ... – not eat (certain types of food)
I keep off spicy foods as they're bad for me.
keep on ...(+ ing) – continue
I haven't found a job yet but I'm going to keep on trying.
keep on – continue giving employment to, not dismiss
How many employees will you keep on at the end of the season?
keep out – not allow to enter
There's an electrified fence to keep out trespassers.
keep up (appearances) – continue to behave as you did previously
To keep up appearances they still go to the best restaurants.
keep up – go at the same speed as
The others were walking so fast that it was difficult to keep up.
keep up – continue, not stop
The snow kept up all day so I didn't go out.
keep up – maintain (payments etc)
I couldn't afford to keep up the payments on the car.
keep up with ... – go at the same speed and stay level with
He had to run faster to keep up with the leaders.

120

keep up with ... – inform yourself of the latest news
I always buy this paper to keep up with the business news.

key in – type something into a computer
She must have made a mistake while she was keying in the data.

kick off – start a game of football (n. kick-off)
The referee blew his whistle and the centre forward kicked off.

kick up (a fuss) – cause a fuss
Mum will kick up a fuss if everything isn't neat and tidy.

kneel down – go down on your knees
The policeman kneeled down and looked through the keyhole.

knock down – hit and cause to fall to the ground
The child was knocked down as she was crossing the road.

knock down – demolish
They've knocked down the swimming pool and built a car park.

knock down – reduce the price (adj. knockdown)
Prices have been knocked down by another ten per cent.

knock out – hit and make unconscious (n. knockout)
He hit me so hard that he knocked me out.

knock out – eliminate from a competition (adj. knockout)
Unfortunately we were knocked out in the semi-final.

lapse into ... – lose concentration and start behaving differently
She suddenly lapsed into the local dialect.

laugh at ... – make fun of, ridicule
They all laughed at his ridiculous costume.

laugh off – pretend something is amusing and not important
Ivor tried to laugh off the incident but he was clearly worried.

lay down – establish (rules, regulations)
You must follow the procedure I have laid down.

lay down – place something somewhere
Can you stop, please, and lay down your pens.

lay down (your life) – sacrifice your life
They laid down their lives for their country.

lay off – dismiss from work (often temporarily)
Times were hard and we had to lay off several employees.

lay on – organise
We hope to lay on some kind of entertainment for the troops.

lay it on – exaggerate
He really laid it on, with all that talk about his rich friends.

lay out – arrange (n. layout)
The garden has been laid out to provide colour all year round.

lay out – spend money (n. outlay)
We've laid out a lot of money to improve the house

leak out (of a secret) – become known
When news of the concert leaked out there was a rush for tickets.

leap at – accept quickly and enthusiastically
We leaped at the chance to make some extra money.

leave on – not switch off
Leave the TV on. I want to watch the film.

leave out – not include
We had to leave out our best player because of injury.

let down – disappoint, not keep a promise
Don't worry. I'll come. I won't let you down.

let down – lengthen (eg a skirt)
The skirt was too short so she let it down.

let down – take the air out of (eg a tyre)
Someone had let down my tyre and I didn't have a pump!

let in – allow in
They won't let you in if you're under eighteen.

let ... into (a secret) – share a secret with someone
I'll let you into a secret. It's my birthday today.

let ... into – allow someone to come into a place
The porter let us into the hotel.

let off – allow a passenger to leave a vehicle
Ask the driver to let you off at the traffic lights.

let off – not punish
I'll let you off this time but don't let it happen again.

let off (steam) – release tension, energy
I told the children to run round the garden to let off steam.

let on – tell someone a secret
It's supposed to be a secret so don't let on.

let out – allow to go outside
Sam opened the door to let the cat out for the night.

let out (clothes) – make clothes larger
When I put on weight, I had to let all my clothes out.

let out ... – emit (a loud noise)
Freddy let out a scream when he saw the snake.

lie ahead – be going to occur in the future
Who knows what further problems lie ahead?

lie down – lie somewhere, usually to rest or sleep
I feel tired so I'm going to lie down for a bit.

lie with ... – be the responsibility of
Who is to blame? - Surely the fault lies with the government.

lift off (of a rocket) – leave the ground
The rocket lifted off and soon disappeared among the clouds.

light up – illuminate
The rockets exploded and lit up the sky.

light up (of eyes) – become bright, excited
Her eyes lit up when she saw the diamond necklace.

line up – stand in a line
Could all the contestants line up in front of the judges?

live down – make people forget a mistake
It was such a stupid thing to do. I'll never live it down.

live off ... – get the money needed to support yourself
He's unemployed so he has to live off the State

live off ... – keep alive by eating
The survivors lived off fish and rainwater for two weeks.

live on ... – have (food or money) for survival
How can I be expected to live on such a low salary?

live on (of a reputation) – survive, continue
Her reputation lived on long after she had left.

live with ... – accept something and continue your life
We all have to live with the consequences of our actions.

liven up – make more interesting and lively
Our host suggested some games to try and liven up the party.

live up to ... – be as good as expected
Vanessa lived up to her reputation as a superb actress.

lock in – prevent someone from leaving by locking the door
I can't get out! They've locked me in!

lock out – prevent someone from entering by locking the door
When I got back to the flat, I found I'd been locked out.

lock up – put in a room and lock the door
The sheriff locked up the prisoner and put a guard outside.

look after ... – take care of, be responsible for
This patient has a special nurse to look after her at night.

look around ... – walk around and look at (a building)
I looked around the building to see what repairs needed doing.

look at ... – examine, check
I'll get a mechanic to look at the engine.

look back – think about past events
When I look back, I still don't know what I did wrong.

look back on ... – think about things that happened in the past
When I look back on those days I realise how lucky I was.

look down on ... – consider inferior
They looked down on her because of her poor clothes.

look for ... – try to find
Excuse me. I'm looking for the police station.

look forward to ... – await with pleasure
I'm looking forward to seeing my friends again.

121

Mini-Dictionary

look in – visit briefly
I'll look in at the chemist's and get some aspirin.
look into ... – investigate
The police are looking into a series of robberies in the area.
look on – watch something happen (n. onlooker)
Julia looked on in horror as the car ran into the shop window.
look on ... – consider, think of someone or something in a certain way
I look on James as someone I can always be frank with.
look out – be careful
Look out! He's got a gun!
look round ... – go around and inspect (a building)
We'll look round the building and see if it's suitable.
look through ... – ignore
That snob looked through me and pretended I wasn't there.
look up – find information in a book
Look up the meaning of the word in this dictionary.
look up – improve
Things are starting to look up. Business is improving.
look up – raise your eyes and look
We looked up and saw the cat in the tree.
look up to ... – respect
I really looked up to my drama teacher. She was my inspiration.
make for ... – go in the direction of
If the alarm goes off, make for the nearest exit.
make ... into – transform
They've made the old theatre into a disco.
make off – run away, escape
The gang made off down the road with the money.
make off with ... – steal and escape with
The thief made off with all the money in my purse.
make out – pretend
The guards made out that they couldn't understand us.
make out – manage to see or hear clearly
It was dark so I couldn't make out the numbers of the houses.
make out a cheque – write a cheque
Please make out the cheque to 'Flowco'.
make up your mind – decide
I've made up my mind to look for a new job.
make up – invent (a story) (adj. made-up)
I'm sure he made up that story about getting lost in the jungle.
make up – become friends again after an argument
Tom and Susan have finally made up after their argument.
make up for ... – compensate for
Tim bought her some flowers to make up for arriving late.
mark down – show that the price has been reduced
Prices have been marked down an extra ten per cent.
measure out – measure (eg a powder) until it is the amount required
Make sure you measure out each chemical very carefully.
meet with ... – have something happen to you
I'm afraid your husband has met with an accident.
miss out – not include
I'll check the list again in case I've missed something out.
miss out on ... – not be involved in (excitement etc)
It's a pity you couldn't come. You missed out on a lot of fun.
mist up – become covered with condensation
The windows misted up and we couldn't see outside.
mistake ... for – think someone is someone else
People are always mistaking me for my sister.
mix up – be unable to tell the difference between
The names are similar so it's easy to mix them up.
mixed up in ... – involved in (something dishonest)
I'm sure that girl was mixed up in the robbery somehow.
move on – make someone move away from a place
The police moved the crowd on to stop them blocking the road.

move on – disperse, go away from a place
The tour party moved on and started looking round the gardens.
move on – talk about something different
Let's move on and talk about the outlook for next year.
move on – make progress (eg to a better job)
Kerry wanted to move on and get a job with more responsibility.
move on to – change to a different subject
They moved on to a less controversial topic.
narrow down – reduce in number by eliminating the others
We've narrowed down the choice to Edinburgh or Athens.
note down – make short notes about
I'd better note down the directions to your house.
open up – talk openly
When Marvin realised I wasn't angry he began to open up.
own up – admit to doing something wrong
If Cathy hadn't owned up, I might have been punished instead.
part with ... – not keep, give or sell to someone
I was very fond of my dog and didn't want to part with him.
pass by – walk past (n. passer-by)
None of the people passing by took any notice of her.
pass on – give someone (a message etc) from someone else
The next time I see her, I'll pass on your news.
pass on (a disease) – transmit a disease
The disease was passed on through the drinking water.
pass on – transfer (the cost or savings)
We hope to pass on any savings to our customers.
pass out – faint
The room was so stuffy that I passed out.
pass over – not consider for promotion
Pratt's been passed over for promotion yet again.
pay ... back – get revenge
Amy's determined to pay him back for embarrassing her.
pay for ... – use money to buy something
Tina's uncle paid for her holiday in Spain.
pay in – deposit money into an account
Have you paid that customer's cheque in yet?.
pay off – pay the money you owe
I should have paid off my debts by the end of the year.
pelt down (of rain) – come down very heavily
The rain was pelting down outside so I decided to stay in.
phase in – introduce gradually
The changes will be phased in over the next few years.
pick at (food) – eat small mouthfuls of food
Robin's only picking at her food. Something must be wrong.
pick out – choose
Try to pick out the smaller tomatoes. They're sweeter.
pick up – learn without much effort
I picked up some of my English by listening to pop music.
pick up – stop a vehicle and collect (adj. pick-up)
The coach will pick you up outside your house at ten o'clock.
pick up (a prize) – win a prize
We picked up first prize in the competition.
pick up (the bill) – pay the bill
Charles picked up the bill. We didn't have to pay anything.
pick up – improve
Sales picked up slightly during the month of August.
piece together – assemble, form a complete idea
We're trying to piece together exactly what happened here.
pile up (of work) – increase
Work really piled up when I was away on business.
plan ahead – plan, arrange things in advance
We're already planning ahead for next year's show.
plant out (seedlings) – re-plant small plants with room to grow
Plant out the seedlings half a metre apart.

play down – make something appear less important
The authorities tried to play down the incident to prevent panic.

play off – play a match to decide who is the winner
The teams had to play off for third place.

play through (a tune) – play a tune from the beginning to the end
Play the tune through so we can hear what it sounds like.

play with (words) – use words to create an effect
The minister was only playing with words. Nothing will change.

plug in – connect to a supply of electricity
Finally, plug in your computer and switch on.

point out – draw attention to a fact or something worth seeing
I must point out that we don't normally work on Sundays.

polish up – improve
I need to polish up my Spanish before my holiday.

pour away – dispose of a liquid
The orange juice smelled strange so I poured it away.

pour down (of rain) – come down heavily
It was pouring down and I didn't have an umbrella.

pour in – enter in large numbers
We expected spectators to pour in but only two thousand came.

pour into ... – enter in large numbers
The doors were opened and the customers poured into the store.

pour out (a drink) – pour a drink into a glass or cup
Give me your cup and I'll pour out the tea.

pour out – reveal feelings in an uncontrolled way
He poured out his problems to his best friend.

print out – print information stored in a computer (n. printout)
Press this key and the computer will print out the details.

proceed against ... – begin legal action to bring to trial
We haven't got enough evidence to proceed against them.

protect ... from – prevent someone being harmed by
Take an umbrella to protect you from the rain.

pull away (of a vehicle) – start to leave a place
The lights turned green and the car pulled away.

pull down – pull something so that it comes down
If the sun is too hot, pull down the blind.

pull in – drive to the side of the road (and often stop)
Let's pull in at the next parking place and have some sandwiches.

pull in – attract
Pop concerts usually pull in a large crowd.

pull in (of a train) – arrive at a station
The train pulled in and the passengers got out.

pull into ... – go to a place off the road to break a journey
The driver pulled into a garage at the side of the road.

pull off – succeed in doing something difficult
Despite all the difficulties she managed to pull off the deal.

pull off – drive off the road
Let's pull off the road and have a rest.

pull off – remove by pulling
I helped one of the riders to pull off her boots.

pull out (of a vehicle) – move into the road or a different traffic lane
A lorry suddenly pulled out into the fast lane.

pull out of ... – decide not to continue
The company pulled out of the agreement.

pull over (of a vehicle) – move to the side of the road
Pull over for a moment and let the other cars go past.

pull through – survive an illness
Nelson was seriously ill but he managed to pull through.

pull up (of a vehicle) – slow down and stop
The van pulled up outside the front door.

push in – get into a queue in front of other people
That woman tried to push in and get on the bus before us!

put away – put something somewhere to make a place tidy
I took the books off the table and put them away.

put back – arrange to have (eg a meeting) later
Can we put the meeting back until the following Tuesday?

put back – return something to the place it was before
Don't forget to put the matches back where you found them.

put by – save for future use
I've got some money put by for emergencies.

put down – kill an animal because it is old or very ill
Our cat was so ill that we had to have him put down.

put down – criticise
People are always putting her down because she's a bit slow.

put down (money) – pay some money as a deposit
I had to put down fifty pounds as a deposit.

put ... down to – give as a reason
I put his bad temper down to pressure of work.

put forward – make a suggestion etc
I'd like to put forward a proposal for improving sales.

put in (a request) – submit, make a request
We have put in a request for a new computer.

put in – install
We've had central heating and double glazing put in.

put in – spend time doing something
The mechanic has put in more than a hundred hours work.

put in for ... – make a formal request for
The manager put in for more staff but the boss refused.

put into words – write or say how you feel or what happened
It's hard to put my feelings into words

put (more effort) into – do something with more effort
You must put more effort into your work.

put money into – invest money in
My son wants me to put more money into the business.

put into ... (of a boat) – enter a port or harbour
The band began to play as the liner put into harbour.

put off – postpone
We've had to put off the match until next month.

put ... off – distract
I can't concentrate. That noise is putting me off.

put off – switch off
Could the last person to leave the room put off the lights, please.

put off – create a bad impression
Don't be put off by his manner. He's really very shy.

put ... off – dissuade (adj. off-putting)
One little mistake shouldn't put you off trying again.

put on – place (make-up, clothes) on your body
Dan took off his pullover and put on a jacket.

put on (weight) – gain weight
I've put on so much weight that I need some new clothes.

put on – present, produce (eg a show)
We're putting on a production of "Romeo and Juliet" next year.

put on – assume, use (an accent, strange face etc)
Fay put on a strange accent and pretended she was a foreigner.

put on (a brave face) – appear cheerful although you are not
Judy managed to put on a brave face despite all her problems.

put it on – try to deceive people
Murray says he's ill but I think he's putting it on.

put out (your tongue) – make your tongue come out of your mouth
How rude! That boy put out his tongue at me!

put out – dislocate (eg your back)
I've put out my back so I mustn't do any lifting.

put out – broadcast
They put out an appeal on the radio for more helpers.

put out (a fire) – extinguish a fire
Cecile used a blanket to put out the fire.

put out – move (an arm etc) away from your body
Mark put out his arm as a signal for the bus to stop.

put ... out – cause someone inconvenience
I hope I'm not putting you out by calling so late.

(I wouldn't) put (it) past ... – I think ... is capable of
I wouldn't put it past her to change her mind at the last moment!

put through – connect someone on the phone
Can you put me through to the manager?

put up – place on a wall
I'll put up a poster on that wall.

put up – give someone food and a bed for the night
The hotels were full so my friends put me up.

put up (a fight) – resist, fight against someone or something
The escaped prisoner didn't put up much of a fight.

put up – increase
Hotels put up their prices in summer.

put up (money) – provide money
My father put up the money to start my business.

put up – choose a candidate for an election
We have to put up a strong candidate for this election.

put up with ... – tolerate
I can't put up with his interference any longer!

quieten down – become less noisy
When the crowd had quietened down, he continued speaking.

rain off (used in the passive) – not allow to start because of rain
The matched was rained off so we had a wasted journey.

ramble on – keep talking in an illogical way
The speaker rambled on about something I couldn't understand.

reach out – stretch out your arm to get something
The shopkeeper reached out and took a tin from the shelf.

read off – look carefully at and note (eg measurements)
I'll read off the measurements if you can write them down.

read out – read in a loud voice
I want you to listen carefully as I read out the names.

reason with ... – try to persuade someone by using logical arguments
We tried to reason with her but she was too angry to listen.

reckon on ... – depend on, expect
You can reckon on at least 40 people coming to the meeting.

remind ... of – make someone remember
This scenery reminds me of the valleys of South Wales.

resign from ... – say officially that you want to leave (eg your job)
Nora resigned from her job after arguing with her boss.

ring ... back – phone (someone) again later
I'll ring you back if there's any more news.

ring off – end a phone conversation
I must ring off now as someone wants to use the phone.

ring out (of bells) – ring loudly
The bells rang out as the couple left the church.

ring up – phone
One of your boyfriends rang up!

rise up – rebel against those in authority (n. uprising)
Finally the people rose up against the dictatorial government.

roll up – make into a cylinder by rolling (adj. rolled-up)
The waiter rolled up a newspaper and tried to hit the fly.

rot away – become rotten and disintegrate
The wood rotted away and the window fell out.

round off – complete an activity satisfactorily
He rounded off the evening with a selection of well-known songs.

rule out – eliminate, not consider
It looks like an accident but we can't rule out murder.

run away – escape from those looking after you (adj. runaway)
The child ran away because she was so unhappy at her aunt's.

run down (of a vehicle) – hit and injure someone
The lorry ran down an old lady who was crossing the road.

run down – lose power
It won't work. Perhaps the batteries have run down.

run down – cause to lose power or effectiveness
They've run down the service. There's only one bus a day.

run into ... – crash into
The car ran into the back of a lorry.

run into ... – reach a figure of
The cost could run into millions of pounds.

run into ... – meet unexpectedly
We ran into difficulties during the test flight.

run on ... – be powered by
This car runs on unleaded petrol.

run out of ... – exhaust, not have any left
I've run out of butter so I'll have to use margarine instead.

run out of (steam) – lose enthusiasm, energy
They started with great enthusiasm but soon ran out of steam.

run over ... (of a vehicle or driver) – hit
The bus ran over a child crossing the road.

run over ... – review, read quickly
Could you just run over the procedure again?

run over – move quickly to a place
They ran over to the shop and looked in the window.

run through ... – repeat (details) quickly for checking purposes
I'll just run through the details of the excursion again.

rush in – enter quickly
The pupils rushed in as soon as the bell rang.

rush into (a decision) – make a decision without thinking
Don't rush into a decision. Think about it carefully first.

rush out – leave a room or building quickly
We all rushed out but the coach had already left.

save up – collect money in order to buy something
I'm saving up to buy a new motorbike.

scale down – reduce the extent of
As night came they scaled down the rescue operation.

scare away – frighten someone and make them go away
The sound of the alarm scared away the thieves.

scare off – make someone too frightened to come near
These guard dogs should scare off any thieves.

scare the pants off ... – make extremely frightened
That horror film scared the pants off me!

scrape off – remove something by scraping
Use a knife to scrape off the paint.

screw up your face – twist your face (to show disapproval)
She screwed up her face in a look of intense disapproval.

seal off – block entrances to prevent movement into or out of a place
The police have sealed off the building so we can't get in.

seal up – close tightly (eg with tape)
Make sure the parcel is properly sealed up before you send it.

see ... into – accompany someone into
A secretary saw me into the office and asked me to sit down.

see off – say goodbye to someone going on a journey
We'll come to the airport to see you off.

see through ... – not be deceived by
The others were fooled but I could see through all his charm.

see to ... – deal with
I've offered to see to the travel arrangements for the holiday.

sell out – sell all the goods in a shop etc
I didn't get any bread because they'd sold out.

send away for ... – write to someone for information etc
I've sent away for details of their autumn breaks.

send back – return something to the place it came from
When Katie got Bill's letter, she sent it back, unopened.

send for ... – send a message for someone to come and help
Marie's condition got worse so we had to send for the doctor.

send in – tell someone to go into a room
Mrs Jones is here. - Please send her in.

send in – write to someone asking for information
Send in for our free illustrated brochure.
send in – send people to a place to deal with a problem
The government had to send in the army to stop the violence.
send off – post (a letter etc)
I need a stamp so I can send off her birthday card.
send off – order a player to leave the field
It was such a bad foul that the referee sent him off.
send on – forward (a letter etc)
Write to my home address. My parents will send the letter on.
send out – send something to a lot of people
We've sent out invitations to all the guests.
set about – start doing something
We'd better set about cleaning up this mess.
set aside (a judgement) – say a judgement is not valid
The judgement was set aside and she was released from prison.
set ... back – cost someone an amount of money
That new car must have set her back at least twenty thousand.
set down (standards) – establish standards
The council has set down standards of hygiene for restaurants.
set in (of a season) – become established
As winter set in, the weather got much worse.
set off – cause something to start
The burglars set off an alarm when they broke the window.
set off – leave on a journey
We're setting off about eight o'clock so we'll be there by twelve.
set off – cause something to explode
We need a volunteer to stay behind and set off the explosives.
set out – start on a journey
The cyclists set out early the following morning.
set out – begin an activity with a specific purpose
We set out to get more people interested in African music.
set out – display in an organised way
The statistics need to be set out in a form that is easy to read.
set up – organise, start
We're going to set up an inquiry into the disaster.
set up (equipment) – place equipment somewhere and get it ready
You can set up the microphones in the corner of the room.
set up a database – prepare a database so that it is ready for use
I've set up a database so that you can make a list of members.
settle down – live a quiet, routine life
She wants her son to get married and settle down.
settle down – become more stable
My headache went and my stomach settled down.
settle into (a routine) – become used to a routine
You soon settle into a routine and life gets quite boring.
sew on – attach, using a needle and thread
Can you sew on this button that came off?
share out – divide and distribute
Share out the rest of the dessert between you.
shave off – remove all the hair by shaving
Burt looks different. - He's shaved off his moustache.
shock ... into – cause someone to do something by shocking them
The horrific accident shocked the council into taking action.
shoot down – bring to the ground by shooting at
A civilian aircraft was shot down by mistake.
shoot up – increase rapidly
The price of petrol has shot up recently.
shop around – go to different shops to find a good price
If you shop around you might find the TV at a lower price.
shout down – shout so loudly that a speaker cannot be heard
Troublemakers in the audience tried to shout the speaker down.
show in – bring someone into a room
Mr Jones is outside. - OK. We're ready. Please show him in.

show off – do things or show things to try and impress people
The girl tried to show off and impress everyone with her dancing.
show out – lead someone out of a place
She showed me out through a side door.
shut down – stop (a machine etc) working (n. shutdown)
We had to shut down the machine as it was overheating.
shut out – not allow to come in
I closed the window to shut out the smoke from the factory.
side with ... – support
In this dispute, I side with the parents.
sift through ... – look through very carefully
We sifted through the list of candidates to find someone suitable.
sign away (your rights) – sign a document giving up certain right(s)
Don't sign away your rights as an employee.
simmer down – become less angry
Once he's simmered down a bit, we'll discuss things more calmly.
sink back into ... – lean backwards deeply into (eg an armchair)
I sank back into my armchair and started reading.
sink in – be slowly understood
As the news began to sink in, people became very worried.
sink (its teeth) into – bite deeply
The dog jumped up and sank its teeth into her arm.
sit around – sit, doing nothing productive
We do all the work while the men sit around chatting!
sit down – be seated (adj. sit-down)
Please sit down and make yourself comfortable.
sit in – occupy a building as a sign of protest
The workers sat in and refused to leave the building.
sit on (a committee) – be a member of a committee
They want you to sit on the housing committee.
sit out (a dance) – sit down and not take part in a dance
I'm very tired so I'd rather sit out the next dance.
slam down – angrily put down something with a loud noise
Tucker slammed down the phone and swore under his breath.
slam on (the brakes) – put your foot quickly on the brake pedal
The driver slammed on the brakes as a dog ran into the road.
sleep through ... – continue sleeping despite the noise
How could you sleep through that terrible storm last night?
slip into (clothes) – put on clothes quickly
Bridget slipped into her dressing gown and hurried downstairs.
slip out – leave quickly and quietly
I'll try and slip out while they're watching television.
slip up – make a mistake (n. slip-up)
These are the wrong tickets. Someone has slipped up.
slow down – go or happen less fast (n. slowdown)
The train slowed down as it entered the tunnel.
smash in – hit something violently until it collapses
We smashed the door in and found the kidnapped boy inside.
smell of ... – give out the smell of
This cake smells of honey.
smooth down – make something have a smooth surface
Giles put some cream on his hair and smoothed it down.
snap out of ... – quickly get out of (a bad mood)
Why is she so miserable? I wish she'd snap out of it.
snowed under – overwhelmed
We've been snowed under with entries for our competition.
soak up the sun – lie in the sun for a long time
I've been soaking up the sun on a Greek island.
sort out a problem – solve a problem
We've got to sort out the problem of where to stay.
spark off – cause a violent activity to begin
The news of the murder sparked off a demonstration.
speak out – not be afraid to give your opinion (adj. outspoken)
People were afraid to speak out on such a controversial topic.

125

speak up – speak more loudly
Can you speak up? I'm a bit deaf.
speed up – go faster
The car began to speed up and was soon out of sight.
spit it out – "Say what you are really thinking!"
Spit it out! Tell us what's on your mind.
splash down (of a spacecraft) – land in water
The spacecraft should splash down in the Pacific.
split up – divide into groups
I want you to split up into groups of four.
split up – end a relationship
How sad! Jack and Jill have just split up after all these years.
spread out – open something and put it on a surface
The general spread the map out on the table.
squeeze out – force something out of a container by squeezing
I just can't squeeze out that last bit of toothpaste!
stand by ... – support
A good friend will stand by you if you're in trouble.
stand by – be in reserve, ready to be used (n. stand-by)
Could you stand by in case we need an extra driver?
stand by ... – not change your mind about what you have said
Nothing has changed. I stand by my original statement.
stand for ... – represent
What do the letters FBI stand for?
stand for ... – tolerate
He won't stand for any nonsense.
stand in – take someone's place (n. stand-in)
You'll have to stand in if he's unable to attend the meeting.
stand in for ... – take someone's place (eg if they are ill)
Jill had to stand in for her boss, who had suddenly been taken ill.
stand out – be noticeable (adj. outstanding)
Eastern Europe stands out as an obvious area for expansion.
stand out (a mile) – be very noticeable
You can see he's jealous. It stands out a mile.
stand up – get to your feet
The pupils have to stand up when the teacher comes in.
stand up for (your rights) – strongly defend your rights
Don't be afraid to stand up for your rights as a citizen.
stand up to ... – not run away from someone
Don't expect me to stand up to somebody with muscles that big!
stand up to ... – endure (rough treatment)
This tower was built to stand up to all kinds of weather.
start out – have as its origin, be originally
This started out as a 96-page book, but it grew!
start up (a business) – get a business going (adj. start-up)
I'm leaving this job to start up my own business.
stay in – not go out
I'm staying in tonight. I've got too much homework to do.
stay on – not leave at the expected time
Many pupils stayed on at school to take some more exams.
stay on – remain in place, not come off
My hat won't stay on in this wind!
stay on – not be switched off
Do the lights have to stay on all night?
stay up – not go to bed
Shall we stay up and watch the late film?
stay out – not return home
Most of the team stayed out celebrating all night.
step down (of a chairperson) – resign
The chairman stepped down and was replaced by his deputy.
step in – get involved, intervene
I had to step in when the discussion got heated.
step up – increase
They had to step up production to meet the increased demand.

stick on – attach, using glue
I'll just stick the stamps on this letter.
stick to the point – not get away from the point
That isn't relevant. Kindly stick to the point.
stick up – point upwards
I hurt my foot on a nail which was sticking up from the floor.
stir up (trouble) – cause trouble
Some agitators tried to stir up trouble at the meeting.
stop off – break a journey
We stopped off in Canberra on the way back to Sydney.
stop over – break a plane journey (n. stopover)
Felicity stopped over in Bangkok on the flight home.
storm out – leave in a very bad temper
Owen lost his temper and stormed out.
stow away – hide (eg on a ship) (n. stowaway)
The boy had stowed away hoping to sail to America.
straighten out – stop someone being worried and confused
This patient has emotional problems. He needs straightening out.
strap up – put bandages around (eg an arm)
The nurse strapped up her arm and told her not to use it.
stretch out – lie at full length
We stretched out on the sand and went to sleep.
strike up (of a band) – start playing music
The band struck up and the dancers began their display.
strip down – take to pieces
We'll have to strip down the engine to find what's wrong.
stub out – extinguish (a cigarette etc) by hitting it against something
He stubbed out his cigarette in the ashtray.
suffer from ... – be in pain because of
When I do a lot of typing, I suffer from terrible neck ache.
sum up – briefly state the main points
I'll try to sum up the situation in a few words.
swallow down – cause to pass from your mouth to your stomach
The pill was so large that it was hard for the boy to swallow it.
swell up (of an ankle) – become larger
If the ankle swells up, put an ice pack on it.
switch off – stop electrical equipment working
Be sure to switch off all the lights before you leave.
switch off – stop paying attention, not be able to concentrate
The lecture was so boring I switched off.
switch on – start electrical equipment working
Can I switch on the TV and watch the news?
swoop down – come down suddenly and seize or attack
The bird swooped down and grabbed the piece of bread.
tail back (of traffic) – form a long queue (n. tailback)
The traffic tailed back for at least a mile.
take aback – surprise
The Government were taken aback by the reaction.
take after ... – resemble
She's very intelligent. She takes after her mother.
take apart – dismantle, take to pieces
I had to take the model apart to fit it into the box.
take (your breath) away – surprise you a lot
The spectacular view took my breath away.
take back – agree that what you said is not true
I take back everything I said. I really enjoyed myself.
take back – return
I must take these books back to the library.
take ... back – make someone think of past events
This dance music takes me back to the time I met your father.
take down – write down information
The reporter took down the details of the accident.
take down – remove from a high place
On the shelf was an old box which he took down and opened.

take down – dismantle, undo something you have erected
I needed help to take down the tent.

take in – fool, deceive
The bogus official was so convincing that he took everyone in.

take in (clothes) – make clothes narrower
When I lost weight, I had to take in all my clothes.

take in – understand everything
I couldn't take in all the information at once.

take in (for questioning) – take to a police station to question
The suspect was taken in for questioning about the robbery.

take ... into (your confidence) – confide in
If we take her into our confidence, will she betray us?

take ... into – accept as part of an organisation
We've decided to take him into the business.

take ... into – accompany someone into a place
We took my daughter into hospital this morning.

take off (of a plane) – depart (n. take-off)
The plane is due to take off at six o'clock.

take off – remove (clothes etc) from your body
Mr Tidy took off his shoes and put on his slippers.

take off – deduct
As a special offer we're taking ten per cent off for new customers.

take off (of sales) – improve considerably
Sales usually take off during the tourist season.

take on – assume (a responsibility, extra work etc)
Are you ready to take on the responsibility of being a manager?

take on (passengers) – allow passengers to board a ship or plane
The plane stopped several times to take on passengers.

take on – give employment to
The company took on five more sales assistants last month.

take out (a book) – borrow a book from a library
You can take out four library books if you want to.

take out – obtain a legal document
Take out some insurance before you go on holiday.

take out – take someone to the cinema etc
He's taking me out to the disco this evening.

take out – extract (eg a tooth)
The dentist had to take out the tooth as it was so bad.

take out (a loan) – arrange to borrow money
She took out a loan to buy a new car.

takes it (out of you) – makes you feel very tired
Doing all this gardening really takes it out of you.

take it out on ... – make someone suffer because you are angry etc
I know you're upset but you don't have to take it out on me!

take over – gain control of (a company) (n. takeover)
The company was taken over by a larger competitor.

take over from ... – replace
Head office has sent someone to take over from the old manager.

take to ... – like someone you meet for the first time
Molly was so friendly that I took to her immediately.

take up – start (a job or hobby)
I took up water-skiing during a seaside holiday.

take up an offer – accept an offer
We decided to take up her offer of accommodation.

take up – use, occupy (time, space)
Organising the meetings was taking up too much of my time.

take up – raise a topic
I'll have to take up the question of overtime with head office.

take up – shorten (eg a skirt)
The skirt was too long so she had to take it up.

talk ... into – persuade someone to do something
Michael's stubborn. You'll never talk him into changing his mind.

talk ... out of – persuade someone not to do something
She tried to talk her boyfriend out of risking his life for her.

tear apart – disturb emotionally, pull in different directions
She was torn apart by wildly conflicting emotions.

tear down – tear off a wall etc
They tore down the old posters and put up new ones.

tear off – remove by tearing
There's a coupon at the bottom of the page for you to tear off.

tear up – tear into pieces
Wanda tore up his letter and threw it out of the window.

tee off – hit the first shot in a game of golf
The first pair of golfers teed off early that morning.

tell ... apart – differentiate between
The twins wear the same clothes so it's difficult to tell them apart.

tell off – reprimand (n. telling-off)
His mother told him off for coming home late.

tell on ... (of pressure) – have a noticeable effect on
The pressure of all the extra work began to tell on her.

tense up – become nervous, make your muscles tight (adj. tensed-up)
I always tense up when I have to make a speech.

think of ... – have an opinion about
What do you think of her latest play?

think over – consider
I'll think over your offer and let you know tomorrow.

think through – think carefully about all the possible consequences
My client needs to think it through. There could be problems.

throw away – get rid of something no longer useful (adj. throwaway)
Throw away any old magazines you don't want.

throw down – throw something downstairs or to a lower position
Your pullover's in the bedroom. I'll throw it down to you.

throw ... into (prison) – force someone to go into prison
Those who opposed the government were thrown into prison.

throw out – get rid of
We had to throw out all the cracked plates.

throw up (a job) – resign from a job
Rosa threw up her job and returned to her country.

tidy up – make (eg room) neat by putting things away
You'll have to tidy up this room before your father gets home.

tie down – limit the freedom of
I don't want to be tied down by a wife and a family.

tighten up (security) – make security stricter
This project is secret so we'll have to tighten up security.

tip off – inform, warn about a future event (n. tip-off)
The police were tipped off about the bank raid.

tire out – make someone very tired (adj. tired out)
Carrying all those bricks really tired me out!

tone down – make less extreme
I had to tone down the speech to avoid a diplomatic incident.

tone up muscles – improve the condition of muscles
These exercises will tone up your leg muscles.

top up – fill up a container that has been partially emptied
Can I top you up or would you prefer a coffee?

touch down (of a plane) – land
The plane had to touch down in the middle of the desert.

touch on ... – mention
The delegate touched on a number of subjects during her speech.

touch up a photo – alter by changing small details (adj. touched-up)
They touched up the photo to make her look much younger.

tow away (of a vehicle) – pull away another vehicle with a rope
The vehicle was towed away after nobody claimed it.

track down – find after a lot of difficulty
I've finally managed to track down a copy of the book.

try on – put on something to see if it fits
I'm not sure of the size so can I try this jacket on?

try out – test
The doctors need volunteers to try out this new vitamin pill.

127

tuck into ... – eat enthusiastically
The hungry workers tucked into their dinner.

tumble down – fall down in disorder
The dog knocked a tin and sent the rest tumbling down.

tune into ... – set controls to a particular frequency, radio station
I like tuning into foreign radio stations.

tune up – make a musical instrument play in tune
The musicians began to tune up as the singers got ready.

turn against ... – no longer support, be hostile to
The people turned against the government after the tax changes.

turn away – refuse entry to
The restaurant was full so we had to turn away customers.

turn back – stop and return the way you have come
The road was blocked so they were forced to turn back.

turn down – refuse, reject
The boss turned down my request for a day off.

turn down – reduce (the heating, volume etc)
If it gets any warmer, we'll turn down the heating.

turn in – go to bed
We'd better turn in soon as we've got an early start tomorrow.

turn in ... – give, submit work to the person who asked you to do it
My students usually turn in very good work.

turn ... into – change into something different
It'll take more than smart clothes to turn him into a gentleman.

turn off – stop an electrical device working
If the red light flashes, turn off the machine immediately.

turn off ... – leave one road and go into another
You have to turn off the road just after the traffic lights.

turn on ... – attack, become hostile
He was badly injured when his dog turned on him.

turn on – start an electrical device working
Turn on the grill and give it time to heat up.

turn on – start behaving in a certain way
Your secretary can certainly turn on the charm!

turn out ... – produce
This factory turns out four hundred bicycles a day.

turn out ... – be in the end
The show turned out to be a great success.

turn out – switch off (the light or gas)
Could you turn out the light when you leave?

turn out – come to a place to see something (n. turnout)
Only a few hundred spectators turned out to see their final game.

turn to ... – go to someone for help
Who else can I turn to if I'm in trouble?

turn up – increase (eg the volume)
Don't turn up the volume! It's loud enough already.

turn up – make something point upwards
The old man turned up his collar as it got more windy.

turn up – arrive, appear somewhere
One cleaner turned up an hour late today.

type away – keep typing
When I went in, his secretary was typing away, as usual.

use up – use all of
We've used up all the paper so we need to order some more.

wake up – (cause someone to) stop sleeping
I usually wake up before the alarm rings in the morning.

walk into a trap – unexpectedly get trapped in a difficult situation
I knew I had walked into a trap when I saw his gun.

walk on – continue walking in a certain direction
Let's walk on and look at some more buildings.

walk out – leave as a sign of protest (n. walk-out)
Half the audience walked out because the acting was so bad.

walk out on ... – leave as a sign of protest
Faith walked out on her husband because he drank.

warm up – do exercises to loosen the muscles (n. warm-up)
We have to warm up before doing the main exercises.

wash down – use water to remove dirt from a surface
You must wash down the walls before you start painting.

wash out – remove as the result of washing
This new detergent will wash out the stain.

wash up – wash the dishes and cutlery (n. washing-up)
The children can clear the table and I'll wash up.

watch out for ... – be careful because of a danger
Watch out for snakes when you go walking in the forest.

water down – make weaker, less controversial
The Minister watered down his speech to avoid giving offence.

wave down – signal to stop
The woman waved me down and asked me for help.

wave on – signal (eg traffic) to continue
The police waved the cars on but made the coaches stop.

wear down – make weaker
The constant questioning was beginning to wear me down.

wear off (of pain) – no longer affect someone
It was some time before the pain wore off.

wear ... out – make someone exhausted (adj. worn out)
Doing all this digging really wears me out.

wear out – wear something so much that it becomes unusable
I've worn out my shoes so I'll have to buy a new pair.

weigh ... down – put someone under a lot of pressure
He was weighed down by all his worries.

weigh up – assess
We must weigh the situation up carefully before deciding.

while away (the time) – make the time pass
She whiled away the time making paper aeroplanes.

whip up – encourage people to feel excited etc
The presenter tried to whip up enthusiasm amongst the audience.

wind down – relax
I need a relaxing hobby to help me wind down at the weekend.

wind down – turn a handle to make something come down
Could you wind down the window so that I can hear you better?

wind down – gradually reduce the amount of work a business does
After his partner died, he began to wind down the business.

wind up (a company) – cause a company to cease trading
Business was so bad that he had to wind up the company.

wire up – connect (a plug) with electrical wires
Are you sure you've wired up that plug correctly?

work away – keep working
I was busy working away and I didn't notice how late it was.

work off – get rid of by exercise
The trainer suggested some exercises to work off excess fat.

work on ... – work to make or improve
Our scientists are working on a new type of plastic.

work on ... – try to influence
I'll work on him and try to get him to change his mind.

work out – think about a problem and find the answer
I just can't work out the answer to this sum.

work out – be all right in the end
I know it looks bad but I'm sure things will work out all right.

work out – do exercises to keep fit (n. work-out)
To keep fit, she works out in the gym for an hour every day.

wrestle with ... – fight with (often morally)
She had to wrestle with her conscience before deciding.

write down – make a note of, record in writing
Have you got some paper? I want to write down this address.

write off – send a letter to an organisation
Simon wrote off for details of their special offer.

write in – insert something into a form or other written text
To save time, I've already written some details in on your form.

write in – write to a TV station etc.
Viewers have written in with more examples of amusing street names.

Answer Key

Here are the answers to all the exercises and the tests. If you are not sure about the answer to an example, try to find it first in the Mini-Dictionary – before looking it up in this key. The Mini-Dictionary gives definitions and examples. Only use this key after you have looked the verb up in the Mini-Dictionary.

Answer Key

PAGE 8 1 set ... off 2 get out 3 broke in 4 put up with 5 rings ... up 6 hold on 7 carry on 8 hung up 9 pay off 10 turn down 11 piled up 12 crack up

PAGE 9 1 set off 2 get out 3 break in 4 put up with 5 ring up 6 hold on 7 carry on 8 hang up 9 pay off 10 turn down 11 pile(s) up 12 crack up

UNIT 1 Ex 1 - 1 put up 2 Cheer up 3 stood up 4 liven ... up 5 build up 6 speak up 7 grew up 8 shot up **Ex 2** - 1 hurry up 2 ring ... up 3 heal up 4 fill up 5 seal ... up 6 locked ... up 7 saved up 8 tidy up

UNIT 2 Ex 1 - 1G 2F 3E 4H 5A 6D 7B 8C **Ex 2** - 1F 2C 3G 4E 5B 6H 7A 8D

UNIT 3 Ex 1 - 1 speed up 2 lit up 3 calling ... up 4 beat ... up 5 pulled up 6 cropped up 7 own up 8 split up **Ex 2** - 1 dig up 2 screwed up 3 polish ... up 4 bottle up 5 tighten up 6 freshen up

UNIT 4 Ex 1 - 1E 2D 3B 4A 5H 6G 7F 8C **Ex 2** - 1E 2D 3F 4B 5A 6C 7H 8G

UNIT 5 Ex 1 - 1 put ... up 2 coming up 3 set up 4 take ... up 5 make up 6 went up 7 picked up 8 give ... up **Ex 2** - 1 take up 2 went up 3 put up 4 set ... up 5 pick ... up 6 give up 7 making ... up 8 came up

UNIT 6 1 pick up 2 give up 3 take up 4 make up 5 set up 6 put up 7 come up 8 go up

UNIT 7 1 keep up 2 bring up 3 turn up 4 draw up 5 look up 6 hold up 7 get up 8 break up

UNIT 8 1 stay up 2 bottle up 3 cheer up 4 own up 5 blow up 6 beat up 7 freshen up 8 dress up 9 mix up 10 brush up 11 screw up 12 back up 13 tighten up 14 crop up 15 dig up

UNIT 9 Ex 1 - 1 Sit down 2 lie down 3 pouring down 4 Slow down 5 chop ... down 6 kneel down 7 blown down 8 shot down **Ex 2** - 1 cooled down 2 calm down 3 tore ... down 4 cut down 5 quietened down 6 fell down 7 marked down 8 tone down

UNIT 10 Ex 1 - 1D 2G 3H 4A 5F 6E 7B 8C **Ex 2** - 1D 2G 3E 4C 5H 6B 7F 8A

UNIT 11 Ex 1 - 1 get ... down 2 Keep down 3 copy down 4 falls down 5 tie ... down 6 wave down 7 water ... down 8 tumbling down **Ex 2** - 1 jot down 2 play down 3 scale down 4 lay down 5 fluttering down 6 narrow ... down

UNIT 12 Ex 1 - 1G 2C 3B 4E 5H 6D 7F 8A **Ex 2** - 1C 2B 3A 4E 5H 6F 7D 8G

UNIT 13 Ex 1 - 1 knocked down 2 go down 3 bring down 4 put down 5 take ... down 6 hold ... down 7 come down 8 turned down **Ex 2** - 1 knocked down 2 take ... down 3 turned down 4 came down 5 go down 6 put ... down 7 hold down 8 bring down

UNIT 14 1 knock down 2 turn down 3 put down 4 bring down 5 take down 6 hold down 7 come down 8 go down

UNIT 15 1 let down 2 fall down 3 get down 4 break down 5 wind down 6 lay down 7 keep down 8 run down

UNIT 16 1 narrow down 2 hand down 3 wear down 4 live down 5 play down 6 settle down 7 pelt down 8 crack down 9 tie down 10 track down 11 tumble down 12 water down 13 wave down 14 climb down 15 jot down

UNIT 17 Ex 1 - 1 walked out 2 jumped out 3 keep out 4 ask ... out 5 cut out 6 squeeze ... out 7 stayed out 8 slip out **Ex 2** - 1 locked ... out 2 rushed out 3 pick out 4 reach out 5 throw out 6 leave ... out 7 eat out 8 check out

UNIT 18 Ex 1 - 1H 2F 3B 4G 5A 6C 7E 8D **Ex 2** - 1D 2C 3H 4G 5B 6A 7E 8F

UNIT 19 Ex 1 - 1 share out 2 camp out 3 try ... out 4 point out 5 stormed out 6 shutting ... out 7 passed out 8 missed out **Ex 2** - 1 Invite ... out 2 cry out 3 hand out 4 wear ... out 5 read out 6 Measure out 7 breathe out 8 stretch out

Answer Key

UNIT 20 Ex 1 - 1B 2F 3E 4H 5D 6C 7G 8A **Ex 2** - 1H 2E 3F 4G 5B 6A 7C 8D

UNIT 21 Ex 1 - 1 take ... out 2 come out 3 put ... out 4 turns out 5 gave ... out 6 let ... out 7 go out 8 make out **Ex 2** - 1 let ... out 2 give out 3 turned out 4 put ... out 5 going out 6 came out 7 took out 8 make out

UNIT 22 1 come out 2 give out 3 let out 4 put out 5 turn out 6 go out 7 make out 8 take out

UNIT 23 1 set out 2 work out 3 carry out 4 call out 5 break out 6 fall out 7 point out 8 drop out

UNIT 24 1 invite out 2 share out 3 stand out 4 hand out 5 throw out 6 spread out 7 back out 8 find out 9 look out 10 pick out 11 cross out 12 cry out 13 storm out 14 pass out 15 burst out

UNIT 25 Ex 1 - 1 came into 2 rush into 3 talk ... into 4 tune into 5 bumped into 6 go into 7 burst into 8 grow into **Ex 2** - 1 check into 2 pulled into 3 put ... into 4 get into 5 looking into 6 let ... into 7 crowded into 8 make ... into

UNIT 26 Ex 1 - 1E 2D 3H 4F 5A 6G 7B 8C **Ex 2** - 1H 2D 3E 4A 5G 6B 7F 8C

UNIT 27 1 run into 2 come into 3 get into 4 burst into 5 go into 6 let ... into 7 take ... into 8 put ... into

UNIT 28 1 bump into 2 shock into 3 check into 4 see into 5 grow into 6 look into 7 fool into 8 walk into 9 pull into 10 crowd into 11 rush into 12 fly into 13 talk into 14 tune into 15 fling into

UNIT 29 Ex 1 - 1 pouring in 2 look in 3 Ask ... in 4 let ... in 5 butted in 6 locked in 7 smash in 8 key in **Ex 2** - 1 stay in 2 drop in 3 join in 4 send ... in 5 fit in 6 fell in 7 pay in 8 push in

UNIT 30 Ex 1 - 1G 2H 3E 4F 5A 6D 7C 8B **Ex 2** - 1H 2F 3D 4G 5A 6B 7C 8E

UNIT 31 Ex 1 - 1 brings/brought in 2 come in 3 got in 4 call in 5 break in 6 fill ... in 7 taken in 8 put in **Ex 2** - 1 put in 2 broke in 3 come in 4 bring in 5 call in 6 fill in 7 take ... in 8 gets in

UNIT 32 1 get in 2 call in 3 bring in 4 break in 5 take in 6 put in 7 fill in 8 come in

UNIT 33 1 send in 2 turn in 3 pull in 4 go in 5 fit in 6 let in 7 give in 8 write in

UNIT 34 1 barge in 2 push in 3 key in 4 pour in 5 step in 6 hand in 7 invite in 8 show in 9 join in 10 drop in 11 phase in 12 plug in 13 smash in 14 sink in 15 stay in 16 pay in

UNIT 35 Ex 1 - 1 Switch ... on 2 looked on 3 stayed on 4 waved ... on 5 count on 6 hit on 7 brought on 8 dragged on **Ex 2** - 1 send on 2 try ... on 3 sew ... on 4 hold on 5 add on 6 live on 7 carried on 8 touch on

UNIT 36 Ex 1 - 1D 2F 3G 4A 5H 6C 7B 8E **Ex 2** - 1H 2A 3G 4F 5D 6C 7B 8E

UNIT 37 Ex 1 - 1 go on 2 get on 3 keep on 4 turn on 5 put on 6 called on 7 come on 8 taken on **Ex 2** - 1 go on 2 called on 3 come on 4 take on 5 getting on 6 put on 7 keep ... on 8 turn on

UNIT 38 1 come on 2 take on 3 call on 4 turn on 5 put on 6 get on 7 go on 8 keep on

UNIT 39 1 move on 2 work on 3 live on 4 catch on 5 bring on 6 stay on 7 look on 8 pass on

UNIT 40 1 ramble on 2 drag on 3 let on 4 carry on 5 count on 6 lay on 7 hold on 8 run on 9 hit on 10 send on 11 switch on 12 leave on 13 touch on 14 try on 15 wave on 16 tell on

UNIT 41 Ex 1 - 1 switch off 2 cut off 3 scare off 4 broke off 5 told ... off 6 show off 7 made off 8 cordoned off **Ex 2** - 1 write off 2 clear off 3 laugh off 4 work off 5 round off 6 fight off 7 pull ... off 8 see ... off

Answer Key

UNIT 42 Ex 1 - 1C 2G 3B 4H 5D 6E 7F 8A **Ex 2** - 1D 2A 3H 4G 5E 6F 7C 8B

UNIT 43 Ex 1 - 1 put off 2 Get off 3 come off 4 set off 5 took off 6 went off 7 turn off 8 let ... off
Ex 2 - 1 turn off 2 gone off 3 (has) got off 4 take off 5 let ... off 6 putting ... off 7 Come off
8 set off

UNIT 44 1 get off 2 put off 3 come off 4 go off 5 take off 6 turn off 7 set off 8 let ... off

UNIT 45 1 break off 2 pull off 3 keep off 4 cut off 5 fall off 6 send off 7 show off 8 switch off

UNIT 46 1 work off 2 cordon off 3 tell off 4 fight off 5 lift off 6 drive off 7 laugh off 8 make off
9 hold off 10 call off 11 wear off 12 see off 13 live off 14 scrape off 15 doze off

UNIT 47 Ex 1 - 1 stand by 2 go after 3 went by 4 takes after 5 came across 6 bring about
7 get by 8 set about **Ex 2** - 1 put by 2 call ... after 3 standing by 4 look after 5 get ... across
6 get by -7 comes across 8 going about

UNIT 48 Ex 1 - 1B 2C 3H 4E 5D 6A 7F 8G **Ex 2** - 1B 2D 3C 4F 5G 6H 7A 8E

UNIT 49 Ex 1 - 1 get around 2 looking around 3 shop around 4 get ... back 5 hold ... against
6 taking ... apart 7 ring ... back 8 take back **Ex 2** - 1 fall back 2 turned against 3 tell ... apart
4 turned back 5 hang around 6 given back 7 crowded around 8 came apart

UNIT 50 Ex 1 - 1H 2F 3B 4E 5D 6A 7C 8G **Ex 2** - 1A 2D 3F 4G 5C 6E 7B 8H

UNIT 51 Ex 1 - 1 deal with 2 go with 3 reason with 4 part with 5 do with 6 playing with
7 fill ... with 8 lies with **Ex 2** - 1 live with 2 deals with 3 met with 4 confusing ... with
5 wrestling with 6 identify with 7 side with 8 disagrees with

UNIT 52 Ex 1 - 1E 2D 3H 4G 5C 6B 7A 8F **Ex 2** - 1D 2F 3H 4A 5G 6B 7E 8C

UNIT 53 Ex 1 - 1 looking for 2 calls for 3 go for 4 made for 5 send for 6 asking for 7 entered for
8 stand for **Ex 2** - 1 pay for 2 went for 3 mistake ... for 4 call for 5 fishing for 6 account for
7 hope for 8 fallen for

UNIT 54 Ex 1 - 1D 2F 3E 4B 5C 6H 7A 8G **Ex 2** - 1G 2F 3H 4A 5C 6E 7D 8B

UNIT 55 1 give away 2 stand by 3 go through 4 call for 5 get over 6 run over 7 get back
8 fall for

UNIT 56 1 get by 2 go by 3 stand for 4 deal with 5 get at 6 go for 7 come across 8 take back

UNIT 57 1 make for 2 get away 3 do with 4 put by 5 see through 6 fall through 7 hand over
8 blow over 9 call after 10 back away 11 pull over 12 set about 13 take after 14 go after
15 while away 16 wrestle with

UNIT 58 1 turn against 2 come to 3 get to 4 hear from 5 jump at 6 dream of 7 shop around
8 tell apart 9 reason with 10 come apart 11 hang around 12 glaze over 13 think of
14 identify with 15 pick at

UNIT 59 Ex 1 - 1 got away with 2 catch up with 3 move on to 4 send away for 5 Watch out for
6 added up to 7 stand in for 8 go ahead with **Ex 2** - 1 look back on 2 made off with
3 walked out on 4 going out with 5 fooling around with 6 cut back on 7 come forward with
8 miss out on

UNIT 60 Ex 1 - 1H 2D 3G 4E 5B 6C 7A 8F **Ex 2** - 1E 2D 3F 4A 5B 6H 7C 8G

UNIT 61 Ex 1 - 1 took ... up on 2 bring ... in on 3 looks down on 4 go on about 5 got round to
6 stand up to 7 go back on 8 done away with **Ex 2** - 1 brought ... out in 2 look up to 3 face up to
4 gone down with 5 make up for 6 go in for 7 break in on 8 took over from

UNIT 62 Ex 1 - 1B 2D 3G 4A 5C 6H 7E 8F **Ex 2** - 1D 2H 3F 4G 5C 6B 7A 8E

Answer Key

UNIT 63 1 get on with 2 feel up to 3 fill in on 4 carry on with 5 look forward to 6 get through to
7 come in for 8 look back on 9 stand in for 10 cut back on 11 break in on 12 get round to
13 fool around with 14 take over from 15 come forward with 16 go down with

UNIT 64 1 look up to 2 go in for 3 run out of 4 look down on 5 go along with 6 grow out of
7 get away with 8 catch up on 9 fix up with 10 live up to 11 come out in 12 cut down on
13 come up against 14 get behind with 15 bring in on 16 get back at

UNIT 65 **Ex 1** - 1 off 2 up 3 out of 4 down 5 down with 6 in 7 on 8 out **Ex 2** - 1 out, in
2 down 3 away 4 off 5 up 6 on 7 in on 8 up to

UNIT 66 **Ex 1** - 1 coming down 2 come in 3 come out 4 came round 5 came across 6 came over
7 coming up 8 come on, came up with **Ex 2** - 1 comes across 2 coming on 3 came into
4 comes from 5 came out in 6 came in for 7 coming off 8 come up

UNIT 67 **Ex 1** - 1F 2C 3G 4B 5D 6H 7A 8E **Ex 2** - 1B 2H 3F 4A 5E 6G 7D 8C

UNIT 68 **Ex 1** - 1 go off 2 went up 3 went by 4 go through 5 go ahead 6 gone down with
7 go down 8 going about **Ex 2** - 1 went off 2 Go on 3 go for 4 go with 5 go into 6 go up
7 going out 8 going without

UNIT 69 **Ex 1** - 1E 2H 3F 4C 5G 6A 7B 8D **Ex 2** - 1B 2F 3G 4H 5C 6A 7E 8D

UNIT 70 **Ex 1** - 1 take back 2 take up 3 taken off 4 take on 5 taking out 6 taken down
7 took ... away 8 took to **Ex 2** - 1 takes after 2 take ... apart 3 takes .... back 4 taken over
5 taken aback 6 taken on 7 take off 8 taken in

UNIT 71 **Ex 1** - 1G 2C 3F 4B 5A 6E 7H 8D **Ex 2** - 1C 2F 3G 4E 5D 6A 7H 8B

UNIT 72 **Ex 1** - 1G 2D 3H 4F 5C 6A 7E 8B **Ex 2** - 1D 2E 3G 4C 5F 6B 7H 8A

UNIT 73 1 keep 2 is 3 look 4 go 5 get

UNIT 74 1 bring 2 take 3 put 4 turn 5 come

UNIT 75 **Ex 1** - 1 close down 2 put forward 3 bring out 4 took over 5 go ahead 6 build up
7 cut back 8 think over **Ex 2** - 1 branch out 2 set up 3 run through 4 sold out 5 take ... up
6 dried up 7 took off 8 plan ahead

UNIT 76 **Ex 1** - 1E 2H 3F 4C 5B 6D 7A 8G **Ex 2** - 1F 2H 3D 4G 5C 6A 7B 8E

UNIT 77 1B 2D 3A 4C 5A 6A 7D 8C 9B 10D 11D 12B 13C 14B

UNIT 78 **Ex 1** - 1 filter out 2 stripped ... down 3 wired up 4 stand up to 5 top up 6 go through
7 reading off 8 cutting out **Ex 2** - 1 print out 2 runs out of 3 set up 4 sift through
5 put ... down to 6 took/takes up 7 worked out 8 back up

UNIT 79 1B 2C 3A 4D 5D 6A 7C 8B 9D 10D 11A 12A 13B 14D

UNIT 80 **Ex 1** 1F 2C 3G 4A 5H 6E 7B 8D **Ex 2** 1H 2G 3B 4A 5D 6E 7F 8C

UNIT 81 1B 2B 3D 4B 5B 6C 7A 8B 9A 10C 11D 12A 13B 14C

UNIT 82 Ex 1 1 1C 2H 3B 4E 5D 6A 7F 8G **Ex 2** 1E 2F 3D 4G 5A 6B 7H 8C

UNIT 83 1B 2B 3C 4B 5D 6A 7A 8C 9D 10A 11D 12B 13A 14D

UNIT 84 1B 2B 3C 4A 5D 6B 7B 8A 9B 10A 11D 12A 13C 14C

UNIT 85 1B 2C 3D 4D 5C 6A 7C 8A 9B 10B 11C 12A 13D 14D

UNIT 86 1C 2D 3A 4A 5C 6C 7A 8B 9C 10B 11B 12A 13B 14D

UNIT 87 **Ex 1** - 1D 2E 3B 4C 5F 6A **Ex 2** - 1D 2F 3E 4B 5A 6CUNIT 88 **Ex 1** - 1F 2D 3B 4E 5C
6A **Ex 2** - 1C 2E 3F 4A 5D 6B

Answer Key

UNIT 89 1 print out, print-out 2 warm up, warm-up 3 burst out, outburst 4 holding up, hold-up
5 broke down, breakdown 6 taking off, take-off 7 dropped out, drop-outs broke out, outbreak
9 stands in, stand-in 10 clean ... up, clean-up

UNIT 90 1 shut down, shut-down 2 (have) brought up, upbringing 3 built up, build-up
4 stop over, stopover 5 taken over, takeover 6 passing by, passers-by 7 stowed away, stowaway
8 stand by, stand-by 9 walked out, walk-out 10 check in, Check-in

UNIT 91 1 got away, getaway 2 hand over, hand-over 3 laid out, layout
4 slowed down, slowdown 5 slipped up, slip-up 6 looking on, onlookers 7 go ahead, go-ahead
8 got together, get-together 9 told ... off, telling-off 10 tailed back, tailback

UNIT 92 1 knocked out, knock-out 2 blacked out, blackout 3 changed over, change-over
4 tipped ... off, tip-off 5 wash up, washing-up 6 rose up, uprising 7 kicked off, kick-off 8 laid out,
outlay 9 working out, work-out 10 (have) turned out, turn-out

UNIT 93 1 rolled up, rolled-up 2 cut off, cut-off 3 ran away, runaway 4 throw ... away, throwaway
5 stands out, outstanding 6 tense up, tensed-up 7 made up, made-up 8 wear ... out, worn out
9 built up, built-up 10 knock down, knockdown

UNIT 94 1 coming in, incoming 2 broke away, breakaway 3 sat down, sit-down
4 start up, start-up 5 touched up, touched-up 6 knocked out, knockout 7 put ... off, off-putting
8 pick up, pick-up 9 tired ... out, tired out 10 speak out, outspoken

UNIT 95 1 turn up, turn ... down 2 passed out, came to 3 stay in, go out 4 set out, get back
5 switched on, switched off 6 knocked ... out, bring ... round 7 slow down, speed up
8 looked down on, looked up to 9 put ... back, brought ... forward 10 stood up, sit down

UNIT 96 1 comes on, goes off 2 started out, ended up 3 step up, cut back 4 take off, Put ... on
5 talk ... out of, talk ... into 6 took off, touched down 7 took ... down, put ... back
8 built up, died down 9 Count ... in, Count ... out 10 break up, go back

TEST 1 1B 2C 3B 4C 5B 6D 7A 8B 9C 10B 11B 12D 13A 14C 15B 16C

TEST 2 1 put 2 turn 3 see 4 come 5 take 6 look 7 sleep 8 go 9 keep 10 come 11 come 12 turn
13 check 14 put 15 look 16 burst 17 miss 18 give

TEST 3 1B 2D 3D 4C 5A 6D 7B 8D 9A 10C 11A 12C 13A 14D 15A 16B

TEST 4 1 come 2 go 3 take 4 weigh 5 come 6 feel 7 blow 8 look 9 put 10 hold 11 rush 12 kick
13 let 14 fill 15 come 16 turn 17 put 18 go

TEST 5 1C 2B 3A 4C 5B 6C 7C 8A 9A 10D 11B 12A 13A 14D 15A 16A

Your Personal List

This book has practised over 700 of the most common phrasal verbs with over 1000 different meanings. There are many more phrasal verbs in English. Use this section to write down and learn other phrasal verbs which you learn in class or while you read.

Try to put your verbs in the best place:

136 – UP   OUT
137 – ON   OFF
138 – IN   DOWN
139 – OVER   INTO   AROUND   AWAY   ABOUT
140 – BACK   FOR   WITH   THROUGH   ROUND
141 – VERBS WITH TWO PARTICLES
142 – GET   PUT
143 – GO   COME
144 – TAKE   BE

Particles – UP, OUT

There are two examples to help you. Add your own.

Why don't you warm		*the meal in the microwave.*	
	UP		

Remember not to miss		*the 'l' in calm.*	
	OUT		

Use this box for a common particle which you need.

Particles – ON, OFF

Write a translation beside the verb if you prefer.

Those silly ideas verge	**ON**	*the ridiculous.*

The Government decided not to break	**OFF**	*diplomatic relations.*

Use this box for a common particle which you need.

Particles – IN, DOWN

Try to write more than just the verb. Write some of the surrounding words.

Wouldn't it be a good idea to trade		*your old car for a new one?*
	IN	

The police tried to crack		*on drug pushers.*
	DOWN	

Use this box for a common particle which you need.

OVER, INTO, AROUND, AWAY, ABOUT

Use this page for verbs with other particles. Write whole sentences.

	The lake froze	**OVER**	*early last winter.*

		INTO	

		AROUND	

		AWAY	

		ABOUT	

Use these boxes for particles which you choose.

BACK, FOR, WITH, THROUGH, ROUND

Write full sentences which make the meaning of the verb clear.

Please ring	**BACK**	*later.*

	FOR	

	WITH	

	THROUGH	

	ROUND	

Add your own particles in these boxes.

Verbs with Two Particles

This page is for you to write the most common phrasal verbs with two particles. Try to write a whole sentence which shows the meaning of the verb.

	PARTICLE 1	PARTICLE 2	
We need to get	**DOWN**	**TO**	*some serious work.*

Common Verbs – GET, PUT

Add a common verb which you decide in the circle at the bottom of the page.
Remember to notice where the particle comes in the sentence or phrase.

GET

over — *a serious illness*

_____ _____
_____ _____
_____ _____
_____ _____
_____ _____
_____ _____

PUT

me up — *for the weekend*

_____ _____
_____ _____
_____ _____
_____ _____
_____ _____
_____ _____

_____ _____
_____ _____
_____ _____
_____ _____
_____ _____
_____ _____

Common Verbs – GO, COME

COME and GO do not have objects. This means that the particle comes immediately after the verb.

GO

up _____   in the world _____

_____   _____

_____   _____

_____   _____

_____   _____

_____   _____

_____   _____

COME

round _____   to my point of view _____

_____   _____

_____   _____

_____   _____

_____   _____

_____   _____

_____   _____

_____   _____

_____   _____

_____   _____

_____   _____

_____   _____

_____   _____

_____   _____

Common Verbs – TAKE, BE

Try to write down phrases which show the meaning of the phrasal verb. Notice especially if the object comes before or after the particle.

up _____ *a new hobby* _____

TAKE

_____ _____

_____ _____

_____ _____

_____ _____

_____ _____

_____ _____

off _____ *my food* _____

BE

_____ _____

_____ _____

_____ _____

_____ _____

_____ _____

_____ _____

_____ _____

_____ _____

_____ _____

_____ _____

_____ _____